Untranslatable Terms of Cultural Practices
A Shared Vocabulary

Untranslatable Terms of Cultural Practices
A Shared Vocabulary

Edition Solitude   Archive Books

Introduction and Foreword

Untranslatable Terms of Cultural Practices

Introduction

Elke aus dem Moore
Denise Helene Sumi
Lara Treffeisen

Kindergarten, *Wanderlust*, *Leitmotif*, and *Zeitgeist* are just a few examples of more than eighty German terms that have been incorporated into the English vocabulary without a translation. A large swathe of humanity has currently »adopted« English as a world language. This leads not only to sometimes crude generalizations and simplifications of language and forms of expression, but also creates new forms of language and understanding. Our language is constantly changing, continuously being expanded. By adding new words to our vocabulary, we become familiar with attitudes and cultural practices, many of which were previously unknown to us.

This book proposes a new vocabulary of terms that remain untranslated in their original language. These are words that represent not only a particular canon, but also cultural practices, attitudes, and value systems. Terms are presented that broaden perspectives, facilitate new perspectives, and thus enrich collective thinking. As an interconnected planetary community, acquainting ourselves with concepts familiar to other cultures is essential. In her contribution to the *Shared Vocabulary*, Simar Preet Kaur, a former Solitude fellow and author, writes:

> Given the awkward consequences of individualism in our hands, a vocabulary for a transformative future would have to lean toward practices that address the species as a whole. Words of inclusion that acknowledge our interconnectedness. Is there a way that langar, as a practice of sharing – and daring, especially in these agitated times – can be expanded with its inherent generosity into a more accessible language?[1]

The terms of the *Shared Vocabulary* are united by their transformative potential. They are meaningful and relevant for imagining new and peacefull interactions with each other. The terms included here convey strategies designed to help readers to perceive the world as radically open and inclusive. In sharing attitudes, value systems, impressions, and observations by the authors, the publication reinforces the idea that a *Shared Vocabulary* can aid us in navigating »collectively.« In the process, the individual contributions are linked and unified by a sense of solidarity and community. This finds expression in terms such as *langar*, *bayanihan*, *gostopriemstvo*, and *mapalus*. *Juogi*, *sahaja*, *cocok*, or *axé* constitute religious or spiritual practices that are based on a cosmological understanding of the world; a sense of community that far exceeds the linguistic, and also integrates nonverbal forms of cohabitation within our processes of thought and emotion, and within our actions. For instance, in its contribution *Anta(h)shira*, the artist collective Raqs Media Collective points out that the social body (and its languages) unites forms of knowledge that do not arise exclusively from our cognitive canon of knowledge, but also encompass emotional and physical aspects:

> We know it when we know it because we know it; in our veins, in our guts, in our bones. And then we never know it alone.[2]

LEARN ANOTHER LANGUAGE [3]

Language can be familiar, can feel like home. Like a favorite dish from our childhood, the »taste« of our native language rolling over our tongue connects us immediately to our roots. We live in a globalized present in which many people use more than one language, and in which questions of nationality also ensure that the concept of the »mother tongue« is a political issue.

Different languages express different aspects of our personality. In her book *Sprache und Sein* (*Language and Being*), Kübra Gümüșay, who also wrote the wonderful foreword to this publication, writes:

> I feel in four languages. [...]
> To me, Turkish is the language of love and melancholy.
> Arabic a mystical, spiritual melody.
> German the language of intellect and yearning.
> And English the language of freedom.[4]

Language is a tool with which we can reveal ourselves to our fellow human beings. However, language, or rather the absence of language, can also divide: The stamps of authority and cultural hegemony have been imposed through linguistic translation techniques and the transmission of speech. Words that are not only part of a particular vocabulary, but also constitute a belief system, continue to be partially denied, thus excluding whole world views and restricting individuals in their cultural practices. By contrast, the *Shared Vocabulary* presents an expanded cultural and etymological understanding within the framework of cultural and linguistic studies sensitive to the context of particular words. This publication seeks to make global knowledge systems visible, while boosting the accessibility of valuable everyday practices.

It seemed important to us to reflect on the specificity of language(s); thus, in his contribution on 信 *XIN* – the Chinese translation principle of authenticity – Dong Li reflects on the problem of untranslatability per se. In it, he refers to Paul Ricoeur, who describes the act of translating as a »work of mourning« and a »work of remembering.«[5] According to Ricoeur, this idea is based on the »linguistic hospitability« of offering a new home to a foreign language – while simultaneously giving expression to a deep appreciation of language and its essence. It is this appreciation of linguistic and cultural translation that we seek to express in this book.

Learning a new language is like falling in love! Acquainting ourselves with the unknown broadens our perspectives and horizons and allows something new to blossom within us, creating fertile ground where transformations can take place.

TRANSFORMATION
30 Years of Akademie Schloss Solitude

The publication mirrors the leitmotif used to mark the 30th anniversary of Akademie Schloss Solitude: *Transformation*. We consolidate the history of the international and transdisciplinary residency program by gathering collective knowledge and promoting transcultural exchange as we highlight valuable concepts of solidarity and sharing practices. The impetus for this publication included the article »Nyantrik as Commoning«[6] by Antariksa, cofounder of the Indonesian KUNCI Cultural Studies Centre in Yogyakarta, which describes a practice of informal artistic education. *Nyantrik* means living together, working together and learning from each other through experience – both artisanal and spiritual. Knowledge only reaches perfection when it is shared, transmitted, and passed on.[7] Concepts such as *nyantrik* (informal artistic education), *gostopriemstvo* (hospitality), or *bayanihan* (mutual support) are also part of the highly unique culture of artist residencies. As a place of community and communal creation, they form a microcosm that can transcend national borders and explore alternative possibilities of cohabitation. In his contribution on *juogi*, a term that describes the deep and multidimensional connection between the world of the living and that of the spirits, cultural journalist Enos Nyamor emphasizes the role of artist residencies and creative and cultural artists as translators and bridge builders between the worlds:

> All musicians and storytellers, for that matter, are considered to be naturally endowed with juogi, for this is the source of their inspiration and what instructs them in their creative processes. When placed in context, an artist residency like Akademie Schloss Solitude would not only be a space for creatives, but also a place occupied by those possessing, or possessed by, juogi.[8]

The authors who share their concepts and stories with us come from different cultural backgrounds. However, they all belong to Akademie Schloss Solitude's international network. They are former fellows, authors, thinkers, scientists, journalists, poets, and visual artists who are connected to cultural practices in different ways. This publication addresses pressing questions with which both artists and scientists alike are confronted: Which value systems are necessary to sustain our living conditions on this planet? What sort of collective wisdom and cultural practices can we learn from as a society? How can we translate this knowledge into sustainable and peaceful action? What can we learn from the Indonesian concept of *gotong royong*, an attitude of solidarity toward a fellow human being in need, or the Japanese tradition of *shinrin yoku*, bathing in and connecting with the forest? And how about *Ubuntu*, the African philosophy meaning »I am because we are« or the Japanese art of *kintsugi*, which cements broken porcelain with gold and thus reinterprets destruction as the potential for renewal?

INCOMPLETENESS INSTEAD OF LITERALNESS

Despite what the term »vocabulary« may imply, we do not intend to constrict the contributions in this publication into a rigid, even lexical form. Instead, we seek to retain the authors' voices in all their heterogeneity. The result is a variety of forms of expression, ranging from poems to stories; from classic lexicon entries to drawings. Besides sharp social observations and well-founded research, the personal stories in particular possess the power to build bridges and convey ideas across linguistic and cultural barriers.

Implicit in this are invariably incompleteness and the mutable nature of language. Different interpretations, fluidity of individual terms, changes in attributions over time due to migration or altered circumstances result in opacity. This book makes no claim to completeness, but also allows space for the unstated – thus not every letter of the alphabet is represented with its own entry. Readers are invited to tolerate the gaps in between, and the irritations and ambivalences that arise as a result. They are an inevitable consequence of cohabitation.

Although it is by no means complete, this publication acts as a guide. It becomes clear that the relationship between language and cultural practice differs from culture to culture. Some cultures cultivate a closer attachment to their languages. Others use it as a tool. In some Asian societies, for example, language seems to be more connected to everyday life and rituals than it is in Europe. How does a living, working language differ from a descriptive, semiotic language?

Many of the terms gathered here are also witnesses to historical entanglements and forced – sometimes violent – migration. The term axé, for example, originated in West Africa and is now part of the vernacular in Brazil. The command *¡Tomá mate!* is couched in the language of Argentina's former Spanish colonial rulers. *Wykombinovać*, *avos'*, *bezmetic*, or *oisiveté* resist the existing social order and describe tactics and strategies for living (or surviving) in the face of communism's restrictions or capitalism's productivity diktat.

A SHARED VOCABULARY

According to Achille Mbembe, cosmopolitanism as a concept constitutes »the idea of a common world, a common humanity, a history and a future that is open to us only if we share it.«[9] It is an invitation to transform this »common past into a shared past« and take responsibility for it, which Mbembe urges us to do. This understanding of a shared past working toward a common future leaves a nation-state mentality and the exploitation of human and natural resources by a few behind, leading instead toward more equitable distribution and mutual respect. A key resource of our thought and action, language can fundamentally express this mutual respect.

The notion of a *Shared Vocabulary* is undergirded by a critical gaze. In order not to lapse into universalism, there is a need to appreciate differences and individual terms and to recognize their contexts of origin. Coexistence takes the place of duality. The aim is not to create a universal lingua franca, a new Esperanto, but to offer an expanded and sensitive view of language and thus of the world, for relationships to each other can only arise through differences, however small.[10]

We would like to note that we have italicized words of non-English linguistic origin only when they first appear in the text and not later. Subsequently, they are sometimes used in upper case and sometimes in lower case in the continuous text, but always without italics.

ACKNOWLEDGEMENTS

We would like to take this opportunity to thank all authors for their insightful contributions. Their writings help to develop a new linguistic self-conception that celebrates language in its diversity and distinctiveness. Thanks also go to the international network of more than 1,500 former fellows and individuals associated with the Akademie, and to all those who have contributed to making this book available in this innovative form. Many thanks to the entire team at Akademie Schloss Solitude.

We would like to thank the funding institutions that made this publication possible, namely the Wüstenrot Stiftung and, in particular, the Ministry of Science, Research and the Arts of the State of Baden-Württemberg, for their unwavering support. Many thanks to our co-publishers Archive Books, especially to Chiara Figone. Thanks are also due to Benjamin Buchegger for the inspiring collaboration in terms of the publication's design, and to Harriet Rössger and Chloe Stead for their meticulous work in translation and editing respectively. We would also like to extend a very special thank you to Kimberly Bradley, one of the Akademie's longest-standing and valued editors.

1 See p. 118.

2 See p. 110.

3 Jessica Martin and Elke aus dem Moore (eds.) *Learn another language*, fanzine.

4 Kübra Gümüsay: *Sprache und Sein*, Berlin 2020, p. 30.

5 See p. 184.

6 Antariksa: »Nyantrik as Commoning,« in: Elke aus dem Moore (ed.), *Politics of Sharing – On Collective Wisdom*, ifa (Institut für Auslandsbeziehungen), 2017, pp. 26–31.

7 This traditional method of knowledge transfer is still used in Indonesia today in a modified form.

8 See p. 24.

9 Achille Mbembe: *Ausgang aus der langen Nacht: Versuch über ein entkolonisiertes Afrika*, Berlin 2016, p. 119.

10 In his essay »Planetary Pursuits,« Shuddhabrata Sengupta refers to Édouard Glissant, who writes »If you forget the tiniest difference in the world, well, Relation is no longer Relation.« Shuddhabrata Sengupta: »Planetary Pursuits,« in: Hildegund Amanshauser and Kimberly Bradley (eds.), *Navigating the Planetary*, Vienna 2020, p. 20.

Foreword

Kübra Gümüşay

Those who live between languages see them. The barriers drawn through linguistic worlds.

Those who live between languages know them. The limitations of translation. The impossibility. It is as if you had to squeeze a whole world through the eye of a needle.

Because when you translate – from one language to another – it is not »just« words for which you seek a counterpart. Instead, you require an equivalent for wide, complex, multifaceted contexts. A perspective. A specific way of regarding the world.

> *Puhpowee.*
> »the force which causes mushrooms
> to push up from the earth overnight.«[1]

When biologist Robin Wall Kimmerer first read the word *Puhpowee* – a word from the language of her ancestors, the Citizen Potawatomi, an indigenous people of North America – she was amazed that such a word even existed. As a biologist, scientist, and botanist, she felt the gap that the absence of this word in other languages created in her, but also in science.

Because what happens when you use the word *Puhpowee*? How do you view the world? In fact, another question seems even more remarkable: *From which perspective* do you regard the world? You look at the world from the perspective of the earth. Not from above, looking down at the plants that grow up to meet you, the human being. But from below, the very bottom. You look at the world from the earth's perspective, up into the sky, past the human beings who constantly believe themselves to be at the very center of the world.

How would we speak differently had we lived in a language that revealed the world to us from the earth's viewpoint? A language like that of the Citizen Potawatomi, in which plants are not spoken of disparagingly as »it,« but rather referred to as respectfully as humans, because they are understood as living beings that also have a perspective on this world? How would our perception change? How would we live differently? How would our relationship with the earth, with nature change?

In an interview, Kimmerer described a situation in which she asked her environmental science students the following question. She asked: *Do you love the earth?*

> They wholeheartedly agree that they love the earth. But when I ask them the question; »Does the earth love you back?« there's a great deal of hesitation and reluctance and eyes cast down, like, oh, gosh, I don't know. Are we even allowed to talk about that? That would mean that the earth had agency and that I was not an anonymous little blip on the landscape, that I was known by my home place.

The language of the Thaayorre in northern Australia is particularly impressive with regard to the perception of space and time. In Kuuk Thaayorre, no words for left and right exist; instead, the Thaayorre use cardinal points, saying, for instance: There's an ant on your northwest arm. Or: Can you please push the cup to the south-southeast? Members of the Thaayorre people can accurately name the cardinal directions even in closed and roofed rooms as early as the ages of four or five.[2] When two Thaayorre meet, they ask each other where the other is going when greeting each other – so the speakers are already encouraged to name the cardinal direction during small talk, which is such an elementary and self-evident part of their language and perception. When Lera Boroditsky tried to learn Kuuk Thaayorre, she experienced the following:

> I had this cool experience when I was there. You know, I was trying to stay oriented because people were treating me like I was pretty stupid for not being oriented, and that hurt. And so I was trying to keep track of which way is which. And one day, I was walking along, and I was just staring at the ground. And all of a sudden, I noticed that there was a new window that had popped up in my mind, and it was like a little bird's-eye view of the landscape that I was walking through, and I was a little red dot that was moving across the landscape. And then when I turned, this little window stayed locked on the landscape, but it turned in my mind's eye. And as soon as I saw that happen, I thought, oh, this makes it so much easier. Now I can stay oriented.

When she told some Thaayorre people about what she considered her strange experience, they laughed and asked how else people should find their bearings in this world.[3]

With its grammatical structures, rules, and norms, our language not only influences our perception of space, but also our perception of time. How does time flow for you? If I were to ask you, as a German or English speaker, to arrange images of a person chronologically from birth to old age, you would probably place childhood images on your left and arrange them by age stretching to the right. In all Latin languages, we write and read from left to right, comprehending time accordingly. Hebrew or Arabic speakers would do the opposite, arranging the images from right to left. But how would the Thaayorre arrange the pictures? The answer is sometimes from left to right, sometimes from right to left, sometimes from front to back, sometimes from back to front – depending on how the subject is sitting at the time. For Thaayorre, time flows from east to west. So if the subject were facing north, they would arrange the images from right to left. If they were facing the opposite direction, they would logically also arrange the images the other way around.

This perception of time and the world had a lasting impression on me. We can only truly comprehend the world view in and with which we were raised when we see it comparatively. Everything revolves around us – indeed around the »I« and its individual perception. I revolve, and so does the world with me. What would it be like if we spoke a language like Kuuk Thaayorre, which constantly reminds us that we are nothing more than a small dot on a huge map; that time flows over us, regardless of the »I« perspective? With what principles, what humility would we regard other people, living beings, nature?

And what happens when these languages are no longer spoken? What do we lose? We lose far more than just words. Far more than *yet another* name for something we all perceive and see. We lose a perspective on this world. We lose eyes. We lose what is beyond the narrow confines of our respective languages.

Like thousands of other indigenous children, Robin Wall Kimmerer's grandfather was taken from his family when he was nine years old and forced to live for years in a boarding school where children were forcibly assimilated and not allowed to speak their native languages. Today, many indigenous languages in North America are endangered, including Potawatomi. One summer, Kimmerer attended a course to learn the language of her ancestors. The language class was eagerly anticipated, Kimmerer writes, because all the living speakers of Potawatomi were expected teach. And they came. On canes, with walking aids, in wheelchairs. Kimmerer counted them: »Nine. Nine fluent speakers. In the whole world. Our language, millennia in the making, sits in those nine chairs. The words that praised creation, told the old stories, lulled my ancestors to sleep, rests today in the tongues of nine very mortal men and women.«[4]

> One of the men told them how his mother hid him when the children were abducted, how he stayed behind as a »carrier of the language.« The man turned to the group: »We're the end of the road. We are all that is left. If you young people do not learn, the language will die. The missionaries and the U.S. government will have their victory at last.«

Then, Kimmerer said, an elderly woman pushed her walker close to the microphone and said: »It's not just the words that will be lost. The language is the heart of our culture; it holds our thoughts, our way of seeing the world. It's too beautiful for English to explain.«[5]

No language captures the whole world. Each language captures it only partially. Each language only grasps and experiences as much as those people who have power and dominion within a language. Each linguistic world only reaches as far as the perception of the rulers and the powerful does. That is why people who wander back and forth between languages are necessary and crucial. People who extend languages, expand them. These are people who – although and precisely because they do not belong to the powerful and ruling class – introduce new perspectives into languages, along with their broad contexts, complexity and richness of facets.

People who know the meaning of *aciziyet: weakness, helplessness*, *incapacity* are the words that automatic translation software offers me when I search for an equivalent of this Turkish word. But *aciziyet* means so much more. A word that makes me look at the world from the bottom up. To feel powerlessness and helplessness, the absence of possibilities, the unattainability of things – and to endure. Yet I don't consider this term negative. There is a strange freedom associated with it. For *aciziyet* also evokes the calm perception of a situation to which a person is exposed. A liberated acceptance of one's life circumstances. Not humiliating inferiority, but respectful deference. Perhaps the prudent, emancipated awareness of our nullity is one of the few truths we can grasp in its completeness. *Our aciziyet*.

To stand at the edge of our linguistic horizon, we must be aware of its existence. *Our aciziyet*. Our dependence on all those people who view the world differently than we do. So that we may be able to stand at the edge of our linguistic horizon and cross it with the help of others; into another language, into words that may not yet even exist.

»*Mapalus* is understood by the indigenous and diasporic Minahasan communities as a form of mutual aid,« writes Natasha Tontey – and thus describing not only a word, but also revealing an attitude to life and a philosophy which places people in relation to each other and to nature. A word that embodies a philosophy that could act as a model beyond the space of this language.

»Micchāmi Dukkaḍaṃ,« explains Nishant Shah, means »May all evil that has been done, be in vain.« Words that are meant to rob evil of its power and strength. They can also mean »I ask pardon from all living beings.« The performative power of language, for both good and evil, is symbolized by this word.

Every word in the *Shared Vocabulary* conveys the power of language, which assumes different forms all over the world.

This vocabulary attempts the impossible. To enlarge the eye of the needle of the languages we speak. To reveal new perspectives from other languages. To broaden our view of the world.

To break down barriers between languages. To free us from their limitations. To recognize humans elsewhere, the »other«, for what they are – human beings.

1 »I stumbled upon it in a book by the Anishinaabe ethnobotanist Keewaydinoquay, in a treatise on the traditional uses of fungi by our people. Puhpowee, she explained, translates as ›the force which causes mushrooms to push up from the earth overnight.‹« Robin Kimmerer: *Braiding Sweetgrass*, Minneapolis 2013, p. 49.

2 The first Western observation of this kind was made by sociolinguist Stephen Levinson, and his research contributed significantly to the more prominent discussion of the linguistic relativity hypothesis in academic discourse. https://pdfs.semanticscholar.org/400c/4086205ebbfacf938478d-5b73ea9eb4b052a.pdf See also Caleb Everett: *Linguistic Relativity. Evidence Across Languages and Cognitive Domains*, Berlin 2013, p. 20.

3 »Lost In Translation,« *Hidden Brain* podcast (January 29, 2018), National Public Radio. https://www.npr.org/transcripts/581657754 (accessed January 16, 2020).

4 Kimmerer: (2013), p. 50.

5 Ibid.

Anta(h)shira

Anta(h)shira
Anta(h)shira
Anta(h)shira
Anta(h)shira
Anta(h)shira
Anta(h)shira
Anta(h)shira
Anta(h)shira

Anta(h)shira
অন্তঃশীরা
Raqs Media Collective

The Bengali word *anta(h)shira* is untranslatable, and uncommon. Except that it is found in specialized »medical« literature and a few obscure Bengali medical dictionaries, where it is taken to mean »intravenous.« This is the sense in which we parse it to capture a shadow of the subterranean forces and flows that shape life. Today, the world needs to draw sustenance, inspiration, and strength from within the anta(h)shira forces in all of us, and to engage in remaking the relationship between the microcosm of the embodied self, and the macrocosm of the cosmos.

It is intriguing and instructive to think of anta(h)shira in terms of a flow that is ubiquitous and subtle, close to and under the skin, but invisible to the naked eye. It is capable of profoundly affecting the body through which it courses, but remains largely misunderstood.

In cultural terms, it could be seen as a capillary conduit for the transit of ideas and concepts in the social body; a transmitter of the mood, or sense, of a time. This may not be immediately graspable or apprehensible, and it may linger, or hover, around utterances, signs, and actions, just as wisps of breath or vapor attach themselves like comic-book thought-bubbles to speech-acts on wintry days; present, but pointing to what else is present, rather than drawing attention to themselves. It is the meaning of what it takes to be the bearer of meaning.

The intravenous flush of warmth that touches the skin for a moment (from the inside) in accompaniment to excitement is anta(h)shira. It may result in the tumescence of expectation or arousal as much as it may signal the need for momentary withdrawal. It can be the secret of the cultural equivalents of goosebumps, of hair-standing-on-end, and of bloodshot eyes. It can contain a spectrum that ranges from the inviting to the combative or protective, from the defensive to the curious, from the camouflaged to the transparent, from the introspective to the extroverted, from the thoughtful to the instinctive, and from the surprised to the surprising. What unites this diversity of responses is the capillary force that acts in each instance, leading to the subcutaneous dispersal of an intuition, a feeling, a hunch or a deliberative sensibility between entities that may be mutually distant, or even ordinarily not in contact with each other.

We know it when we know it because we know it; in our veins, in our guts, in our bones. And then we never know it alone.

Sometimes, such as when we sense that something fundamental has shifted, we feel the anta(h)shira manifest. It brings into awareness the latent flux between many. It precipitates the surge of sense and sediment from the reservoirs of that which is in common. This can happen when an encounter with a quiet but determined gesture, an utterance transmitted word-of-mouth, or an orphaned sign (of which we may know neither provenance nor parentage) becomes a catalyst for a contagious series of transformations in the consciousness of a city's inhabitants. Nobody can claim authorship of such a moment but everyone can make it their own.

At other times, it rises in us like a tidal bore swelling to the pull of a celestial force; something that we know will keep us awake at night until we step out into the uncanny radiance of moonshine or nightshade, and find ourselves in the company of other joyful or disturbed insomniacs.

Like many things subcutaneous, the anta(h)shira may be misunderstood as being »dormant.« Just because it lies under the skin does not mean that it is buried. It remains alive and in reserve. In a majority of instances, the reality that we are referring to is hibernating, or, on a different temporal register, »power-napping,« conserving its energies, waiting for a serendipitous moment when it can unfurl itself to its fullest extent. Until that happens, it courses through the arteries as potential, waiting to be called upon. Meanwhile, it learns new things through the porosity of veins.

The anta(h)shira bides its time to flood.

USAGE

· Her words, otherwise thought lost, were protected and kept alive within the flow of anta(h)shira. They reappeared, after a few centuries, with a new force.

· The *Annihiliation of Caste*, both as text and as idea, was kept aglow over the last seven decades – in spite of dominant amnesia – in the anta(h)shira of millions.

Avos’
Avos’
Avos’
Avos’
Avos’
Avos’
Avos’
Avos’

Avos'
Viktoria Morasch

Avoska, 2020, photo: Julia Brenner
Courtesy of the photographer

Just a net with two handles made of plastic or cotton. So small it can disappear in your pocket. And yet, if the conditions are right, it expands to surprising dimensions. The typical Soviet string bag, the *avoska*, is the concretion of a rather abstract concept – *avos'*.

The avoska is a bag that you take with you when you go out. Shopping in today's sense didn't exist in the Soviet Union, because you couldn't plan on buying anything. You took your avoska and if you were lucky – if you stood long enough in line – there was maybe something for you in the shop. Milk, butter, bread, potatoes. The avoska would perfectly adapt to size and weight. And if there was nothing you could bring home to your family, the bag discreetly disappeared into one of your pockets.

Avos' is said to be crucial to Russian mentality and is therefore impossible to translate. Just like the bag, avos' means optimism in harsh circumstances. It is an attitude, a behavior passed from generation to generation. Because some things never change: Russian people suffer. They suffer from politics, weather, and gloom. Avos' makes sense of the suffering. It means believing that the suffering is not in vain, and all sorrows can be overcome. Or, as every Russian mother says: everything will be fine.

Contrary to the Western notion of overcoming hardship or misery, the Russian approach is rather passive. It is based, I think, on the feeling of having limited power, the understanding of life being unpredictable and a tendency toward superstition. Avos' means being hopeful without reason. It means ignoring problems, looking the other way and focusing on something less earthly, on the good things that might happen despite all rational doubts. When you have been governed by czars, dictators, drunkards, and corrupted autocrats, when worldly structures have mostly been there to exploit you – you turn to sheer luck. But then again, it's more than luck. It's optimism and fatalism at the same time. It's the resilience that says that it might as well turn out well for me (even though there are no indications of that).

Avos' can be used as a particle or a noun. The particle means something like »hopefully« or »maybe« in the atheistic sense of »if God wills.« The noun means what I tried to explain above: blind faith and likable naïveté paired with often less likable passivity. For example, the sixteen-year old patient in Aleksandr Solzhenitsyn's novel *Cancer Ward* refuses an operation saying »Hope (avos') it'll be resolved on its own.« His friend answers: »It is stupid to think that you can build a bridge on avos'.«

Avos' is an alternative to likeliness. Believing in it can lead to risky decisions, economic speculations, and falling for scams. It means buying a house from a shady construction firm, not checking its background, paying in advance and hoping that its system would collapse just after your house was built. It means signing a contract because the office is on your way home. It means getting engaged to someone who beats you and hope he will stop once you are married. It means giving your life savings to your junkie neighbor because he promised an extremely profitable investment. It means not doing your homework and hoping the teacher will not ask for it.

Acting according to avos' doesn't have much to do with the Western notion of laissez-faire because laissez-faire assumes that there are some kind of rules and laws. Avos' does not. It comes from a world where not abiding by the rules means success, and abiding by them means failure.

There are many sad cases of avos'. Even Vladimir Putin recently urged his people to be responsible and stop relying on it to cope with the coronavirus pandemic. And yet, there are also beautiful examples of avos' – because the word stands for disruption and surprise, and for something deeply human: hope against all odds.

Axé

Axé

Axé

Axé

Axé

Axé

Axé

Axé

Axé

Axé

Vinicius Jatobá

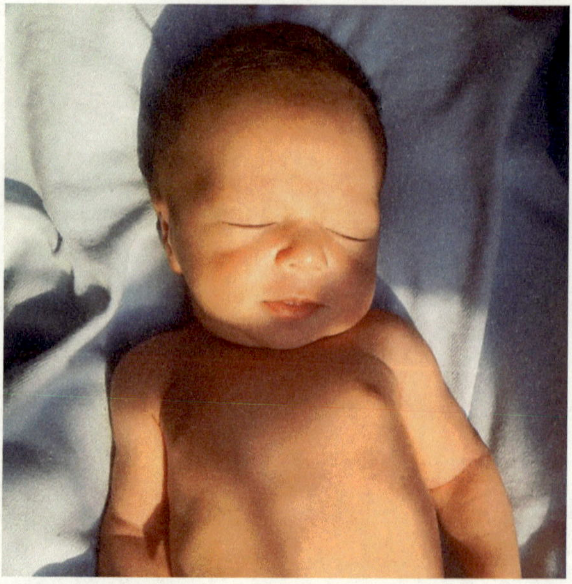

Photo: Vitor Jatobá
Courtesy of the photographer

Axé is a religious word that comes from West Africa. It originates in the Yoruba language, and is an important concept to the practices and beliefs of the Candomblé and Umbanda religions. But its presence in the Brazilian conscience goes beyond these religions; Axé is widely used in our vernacular. Axé is used when desiring good things for beloved ones, cherishing opportunities, and communicating with the beyond.

LASTING BLESSINGS

When my great-grandmother looked at my grandfather
that morning
If she only knew it was his last morning on Earth,
if she knew
As she was his mother, my great-grandmother, sewing
dresses daily
And it was unfair for a woman to so suddenly bury
the bosom of her womb
Only if she knew that this was his last morning, his last
morning on Earth
But not the very last of his presence for me, a small
child listening
His lores and adventures, playing with the grandfather
I never knew
While my great-grandmother, his mother diligently
sews new dresses

(Now old and ancient, dusty and non-existent, four decades ago)
She probably would have had said to him *Axé on your new path*
So much Axé for you on your new path, don't look back I'll join you
Once I sew all the dresses I still have to sew, my beloved son.

My mother hugged me before I boarded the plane that flew me to Europe
And she said *Axé* as in *don't be afraid the world is big but not so big*
That you will not hear me speaking to you when you don't know
What to do and I told her *Axé* as in *I'm sorry I'll not be with you tomorrow*
And by tomorrow I mean the decades that I'll exist after she's gone.

. . .

If ever one person could sing to me as honestly as the Black Forest birds
When in afternoons of loneliness I feared the certainty of my parents' death
I could assume in the heart of the pandemic that such a world is still livable
Even when all had stopped: *Axé the spirit that still looms when the world stands still.*

And my mother will not die as she can't die as she is my
mother, smoking
The coronavirus will just crown her head and steal her
breath and give her fever
But my mother is too busy to die now, the silence of
the Black Forest commutes.
And after so much work my mother has the right to be
a tiny old lady still smoking
Still smoking and gazing, gazing at the wonders of all
awfulness that was not that bad
*Life wasn't that bad and there is more misery to come
my darlings*
*There is so much more to come and the world has not
even begun.*

. . .

Once a century it seems a pandemic comes and kills the
beloved ones
So all those surviving can go on forgetting them generation
after generation
Until the next pandemic makes a writer remember
the last pandemic
As every family from century to century produces not just
bones but words.

The writer will come and kill the family by writing
whatever wasn't spoken

All the tiny dirty little naked secrets that loomed in the dark, also smoking
Or even sewing, for that matter, as I could hear in my childhood her murmur
My great-grandmother sitting at the sewing machine murmuring guilty words
Saying *I'm sorry* from time to time saying *I'm so sorry* from time to time
Saying *I'm so very sorry* from time to time *I'm so terribly sorry*
And so four times she was sorry as there were four great brothers, stallions
That she lost in 1920 to the Spanish Flu, one after another in a week's span.

When my great-grandmother went to her son's burial she must have thought
Thanks for the Axé of giving me the opportunity of finally burying all of them
As I have to give back to the same land what I love the most my own son
So my brothers understand just now what I understood as a young girl
That you will lose love regardless so hold tight, just hold tight, tighter
But not tight enough so your own palms are the reason for their demise.

I learned early that the soul speaks to beans, as each bean
is a soul
And a soul so bright you could even imagine that the calm
temperate stars
Are white beans floating over a very dark moody mushy sea
So I cooked them with care, with the utmost care,
because on some days
A child would be born, the son of my brother now a father,
scared
Because a small enchanted piece of flesh will yell and cry
for love
His love, and his love, an Axé hugging another Axé, his child.

So many doors will be opened with the gaze of this child,
I thought cooking
The beans that are soft and smooth and became even more
soft and smooth
Because a kid was there rehearsing for his premiere:
studying his lines,
Looking at the aquatic mirror of the womb's flesh, deep
swimming,
All these lines crafted and studied that he would merrily
forget
The very moment he's born, so we would think he's learning
from us
All that fate has already carved into his path and mind
and soul.

Bayanihan
Bayanihan
Bayanihan
Bayanihan
Bayanihan
Bayanihan
Bayanihan
Bayanihan

Bayanihan
Mica Cabildo

Balsa (Rafts), Akiyoshidai/JP, 2019, photo: Mica Cabildo
Courtesy of the artist

A Visayan creation myth documented in the Boxer Codex (ca. 1590) tells of an ancient quarrel between the sea and the sky, incited by a cunning bird of prey. The sea lashed waves against the sky, and the sky threw rocks and islands at the sea. Finally, the bird, tired of flying, found some earth to rest upon. However, the bird's peace was short-lived, disturbed by a length of bamboo that washed back and forth upon the island. Annoyed, the bird pecked furiously on the bamboo stalk until it split, revealing a curious sight. A sturdy brown creature slept in the stalk's first node, while from the second node a supple creature with long, black hair stepped out. And so the first man and woman appeared on earth.[1]

In the hills surrounding the Akiyoshidai International Art Village, bamboo trees grow to seven meters tall and twenty centimeters wide. To cut one down you need a chainsaw and an experienced person to operate it; three more people would carry each forty-kilogram pole down a muddy slope and over a narrow canal. You would do this sixty times. The seven-meter poles are inspected, cut into three-meter lengths with a table saw, transported to the concert hall through the piano lift, and carried piece by piece onto a flat staging area before the courtyard. With thick wara rope, the bamboo pieces are tied together into five large, heavy rafts. Finally, eight able-bodied men carry each raft into place, stumbling on the smooth rocks of a dried up fountain. Someone asks, »Are we building a house?«

Bayanihan is the Tagalog word for cooperative action, first defined in 1754 as *obra cómun* (common work) or *ser juntado para la obra* (to be gathered for the work).[2] Its root words *bayani* (one who acts selflessly) and *bayan* (a place and its people) can be traced back to the Austronesian word *bahay* (house) and its collective *bahayan* (community of houses). Irrigation-based agriculture and stable trade resulted in the establishment of permanent *bahayan* and led to the development of the *bayan* ethnic state. In the bayan, bayani was a specialized sociopolitical class tasked with the physical defense of the community.[3]

Central to these pre-Hispanic communities was an animist native religion, *anito*. In the world of anito, the living exist on the same plane as unseen spirits of the dead, who may help those who are sick, lost, or in danger. The ritual worship of anito was a communal responsibility, and any individual's wrongdoing could bring about punishment upon the entire community. In these egalitarian societies, bayanihan was understood as cooperation without expectation of reward.[4]

Later on, bayanihan was expressed as unpaid farmwork carried out among relatives and neighbors, who collectively shared in the labor and gains of planting and harvesting. This interdependency enabled each member of the community to meet their needs and survive without money.[5]

Within the Filipino value system, the basis of all relations and social interactions are the concept of *kapwa* (shared self) and the core value of *pakikipagkapwa* (human concern and interaction as one with others). *Kapwa* is an awareness of shared identity or being »together with a person,« of having the same nature and being of equal status, while pakikipagkapwa is the conviction and moral standard of relating to one another as fellow human beings. It is within this unique value system that bayanihan is embedded.[6]

Carlos V. Francisco's iconic mural *Bayanihan*, commissioned by drug manufacturer Unilab in 1962, shows a pastoral scene of rural folk carrying a bamboo hut on their shoulders as they help a neighbor relocate.[7] Former Philippine President Ferdinand Marcos evoked the same imagery in his ideology for a New Society »rooted in the bayanihan spirit exemplified by neighbors and friends who help out in transplanting a house.«[8] Ferdinand and Imelda would be Father and Mother to this New Society, and in further acts of myth-making had even commissioned painters to depict them as Malakas (the Strong One) and Maganda (the Beautiful One) – the first man and woman of the archipelago, sprung out of a split bamboo stalk.[9]

»Are we building a house?«

Five large bamboo rafts lay stranded in the Akiyoshidai International Art Village courtyard, waiting for the tide to come back in. The karst plateau was once a vast underwater coral reef, much like the Palawan microarchipelago in southwestern Luzon. In a thousand years, when the sea returns to Akiyoshidai, such rafts built through bayanihan might serve as temporary houses to transplant and relocate similar bodies that carried them into place.

In the Philippines, the ancient quarrel between the sea and the sky rages on, and the myth-making behind bayanihan continues into the twenty-first century. Bayanihan is evoked whenever collective action is needed. Disaster studies scholar Greg Bankoff cites bayanihan as a culturally specific coping practice that »guarantees support for members, especially during times of personal travail or common hardship.«[10] However, studies undertaken on bayanihan in the aftermath of Typhoon Haiyan in 2013 reveal that post-disaster resilience and bayanihan were myths: while bayanihan activities were observed immediately after the disaster, lack of transparency and unequal distribution of aid eroded trust and bayanihan within the affected communities.[11]

In such times, a good question to ask would be, »Whose house are we carrying?«

To which the only acceptable answer would be, »Does it matter?«

The bamboo rafts in Akiyoshidai have since been dismantled without mythicization or romance. Neither man nor woman sprung out of the stalks, which were simply returned to the hills where they were sourced. Young bamboo shoots growing from stumps of cut stalks would serve as food in the spring; decaying stalks would provide organic matter for sprouting mushrooms when the rains come. Within the safe walls and egalitarian self-organization of the international artist residency, all would share in the gains of the harvest in the same way that they shared in the labor of building.

1 Jordan C: »Examining the ›First Man & Woman from Bamboo‹ Philippine Myths,« Aswang Project, June 15, 2020, https://www.aswangproject.com/malakas-maganda-myth/.

2 Juan José de Noceda and Pedro de Saluncar: *Vocabulario de la Lengua Tagala*, eds. Virgilio S. Almario, Elvin R. Ebreo and Anna Maria M. Yglopaz. Manila 2013, p. 72.

3 Ma. Corazon J. Veneracion: »Bago dumating ang social work: Ang katutubong konsepto ng pagtutulong sa Filipinas,« *Daluyan* 12, no. 1 (2004), p. 104.

4 Ibid., p. 109.

5 Amaryllis T. Torres: »Kinship and Social Relations in Filipino Culture,« in: *Sikolohiyang Pilipino: isyu, pananaw at kaalaman*, eds. Allen Aganon & Ma. Assumpta David. Manila 1985, pp. 488–95.

6 F. Landa Jocano: *Filipino Value System: A Cultural Definition*. Metro Manila 1997; Virgilio G. Enriquez: »Kapwa: A Core Concept in Filipino Social Psychology,« in: *Philippine World-view*, ed. Virgilio G. Enriquez. Singapore 1986, pp. 6–11; Jeremiah Reyes: »Loób and Kapwa: An Introduction to a Filipino Virtue Ethics,« in: *Asian Philosophy* 25, no. 2, 2015: p. 156, https://doi.org/10.1080/09552367.2015.1043173 (accessed November 25, 2020).

7 Unilab: »The Bayanihan Mural,« March 07, 2012, Facebook, https://www.facebook.com/Unilab/posts/10150576023930829 (accessed November 25, 2020).

8 Ferdinand E. Marcos: »The True Filipino Ideology,« in: *Speeches by President Ferdinand E. Marcos. Manila* 1982, https://www.officialgazette.gov.ph/1982/05/12/essay-by-president-marcos-entitled-the-true-filipino-ideology/ (accessed November 25, 2020).

9 Marco Sumayao: »Painting the Marcos Myth with Ferdinand as Malakas, Imelda as Maganda,« in: *Esquire Philippines*, September 24, 2018, https://www.esquiremag.ph/culture/lifestyle/marcos-malakas-maganda-a2239-20180924-lfrm (accessed November 25, 2020).

10 Greg Bankoff: *Cultures of Disaster: Society and Natural Hazard in the Philippines*. New York 2003, pp. 168–80.

11 Yvonne Su and Maria Tanyag: »Globalising myths of survival: post-disaster households after Typhoon Haiyan,« in: *Gender, Place & Culture: A Journal of Feminist Geography* 27, no. 11, 2019: 18, https://doi.org/10.1080/0966369X.2019.1635997; »Bayanihan After Typhoon Haiyan: are we romanticising an indigenous coping strategy?« in: *Humanitarian Practice Network*, August 10, 2016, https://odihpn.org/blog/bayanihan-after-typhoon-haiyan-are-we-romanticising-an-indigenous-coping-strategy/ (both accessed November 25, 2020).

Bezmetic
Bezmetic
Bezmetic
Bezmetic
Bezmetic
Bezmetic
Bezmetic
Bezmetic
Bezmetic
Bezmetic
Bezmetic

Bezmetic
Edith Lázár

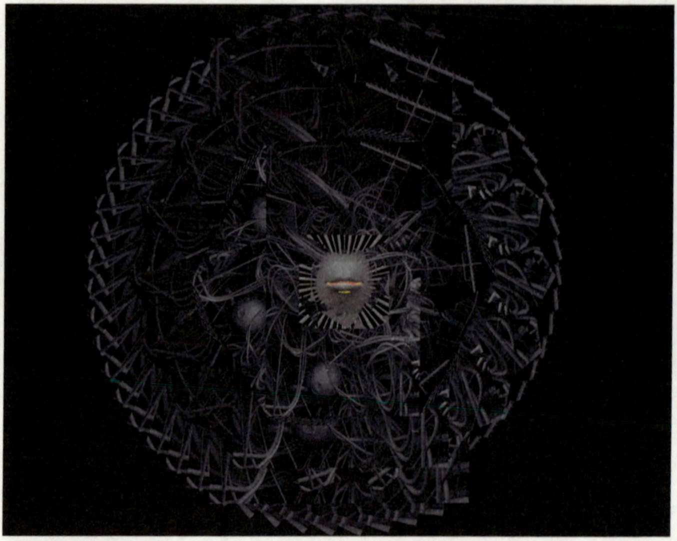

Taietzel Ticalos, *The pervasive sense of passage*, 2020
Courtesy of the artist

Bezmetic is moving, and it's dizzying. The word denotes neither a lunatic nor a mad person, but someone who moves around in a dazzling way. Not running around without purpose, either, yet a bezmetic manifests an unquiet disorder in its pursuit. Bezmetic is a drunkenness of sorts, one that is only perceived as such and pointed out by others. »Why are you spinning around like a bezmetic?« would be the most common phrasing.

Bezmetic itself is a rather unusual word in Romanian, proving difficult to pin down. Its provenance has been sub-ject to debates, with both its use and formation shifting between its Slavic inflections – a trait of the Balkan region – and such modulations in our otherwise Latin language. From the Slavic root *bezŭ matokŭ*, it suggests a beehive wandering around without a queen (matca), whereas the Latin hypothesis derives it from *amphisbeticus*, as »quarrelsome« or litigious. And then, it could be neither. Common parlance blends everything and adds more, making bezmetic noisy, dazzled, dazzling, dizzying, and incomprehensible. »Out of the perimeter« or habits, perhaps. Human and non-human at once.

The reader might well wonder what makes then such a confusing word a subject of attention. And subject it is, rather than an object, as bezmetic resists proper translation by being primarily a visual and bodily manifestation, a dynamo spreading and weaving other connections on its way. And thus, instead of looking at the word itself, we might need to look at something else.

In our abundant folklore, unspoken ties that bind humans to magic – of an utmost organic nature – permeate words and speech. The »mistresses of the wind/ladies of the earth and mist« are, perhaps, renowned for such unruly forces. Similar to naiads, young nymphs, the iele are »mysterious beings« who can without any warning punish or make fun of those with the audacity to ignore their unwritten boundaries. In local mythologies, they can make one from human to un-human (*pe dată îl fac din om neom*) – an »illness« often causing aimless wandering and temporary loss of speech. Some male ethnologists have cast them as ensnaringly young girls or »she-devils,« often binding young men. But in stories, the iele are neither good nor evil. Rather, their lost items are endowed with healing powers, and they tend to seek revenge only when provoked.

Language ... still the most draconian of instruments through which we subjugate the ineffable and the sensible, giving it a place, a form, a naming – making it fit an order. Not being able to speak it out or see it out, in order to place a place or name a name, can then be seen as a manner of resisting ruling structures; just as wielding the words high up in fictions (as if by magic) can unhitch them from their prior meaning.

Somehow, bezmetic seems to elude the »rational« order and the empire of reason, which haven't proved so reasonable anyway. It is precisely reason that has imposed violent and restrictive normalcies on what individuals should be, measuring and ordering us around. Out of this, we can sense that bezmetic was pointed at those refusing normative behavior – sexuality and gender included – as if »they don't know what they're doing,« as if they are failing an order. It shares this trait from the old Slavic words, *bezokij* – someone lacking a clear vision; and *bezaku*, the improper, or disorderly, as lack of conduct.

Worth mentioning is that until the nineteenth century, the prefix bez- circulated as a word in itself, meaning something that shouldn't be counted; and then got paired with *dezmetic* – to come to one's senses. But bezmetic stands most closely to *bezna* (the darkness or pitch black), the abyss of the vast marine space or the celestial one, the unknown universes resting in the corners of our eyes. Although bezmetic touches upon blind spots, it is only as a temporary state, carrying the promise of arriving at a shore. Yet, like magical thinking, it's not back to consciousness, but into it. And just like the »order« the wandering beehive returns to, it's never the same, even if we idealize it as such. Neither is the »order« to which a person returns.

And now that we are about to get back to *the hive*, we're confronted with more threads. Could this be an artificial connection: »is the word used only for the honeybees, or is it used regardless of anything else?« As it turns out, the word's main use does concern honeybees, as in everyday speech its transfer to »something else,« concerns mainly people. This transmutation holds little to no surprise. Honeybees have lived a long life as sociopolitical animals among humans. The bees became a utopic repository for community, collective care, and labor – the ultimate worker working »not for one alone, but for all its fellows.« So strong is this image that, when an eighteenth-century philosopher dared to suggest that bees are as vice-addled as humans, his book was publicly burned. Even our tech-infused language uses terms like hive-mind for horizontally built software or models of distributed intelligence, and swarm for the technicalities of algorithms. As through the looking glass, bezmetic appears as a knowledge »out of stupular thought,« an immersion into something that silently resists such structures.

If we are to thus envision arches from one to another, being bezmetic can be a practice in (dis)order, one of many ties that can bind, since it holds a galvanizing force. Bezmetic wanderings are both pre- and unsettling. They cast away the »rational« order not by opposing it, but by just not »seeing« it. As temporary states, they are able to make space, bodily and affectively, collectively as well, for other perimeters; and do so from a vulnerable place, where knowing and not-knowing are not hierarchical delimitations.

1 Andrei Oișteanu: *Motive și Semnificații Mito-Simbolice în Cultura Românească*, Bucharest 1989, pp. 201–02.

2 Andreea Bargan: »The Probable Old Germanic Origin of Romanian *lele* (evil) fairies,« in: *Messages, Sages and Ages*, 2 (2), 2015. DOI: 10.1515/msas-2015-0007

3 Sergiu Drincu: »Prefixe Românești de Proveniență Slavă (2)« in *Philologica Banatica*, Vol. 2, Timișoara 2014, pp. 80–81.

4 See *Bezna* as a tool for speculative thinking and Alina Popa and Florin Flueras »The Second Body« (the peripheral body and thinking with the unknown). Available online at http://bezzzna.blogspot.com/2013/06/bezna-4.html (accessed November 17, 2020).

5 Drincu, p. 82 (see note 3).

6 Mariana Silva: »The Insect Wing of the Museum of Social Forms,« in: *Matter Fictions*, Berlin 2017, pp. 101–02. Silva notes that from Aristoteles to Karl Marx, or recent anthropology studies, honeybees have been domesticated into »natural« models of order and collectivity serving varied regimes, including the constitutional monarchy or liberal democracy. The »outrageous« book *Fable of the Bees* was written by Bernard Mandevill.

* I would like to thank Flaviu Rogojan for drawing my attention to bezmetic's erratic meanings.

Cocok
Cocok
Cocok
Cocok
Cocok
Cocok
Cocok
Cocok
Cocok
Cocok
Cocok

Cocok
Laura Romano

Cocok is an Indonesian word of Javanese origins. If you look it up in the dictionary, it has many meanings indeed.[1] It means fitting, suitable, just right, similar, identical, in accord, compatible; to agree, tally, jibe, correct, right, precise, exact, fitting, to appeal strongly, to be to one's taste, suit.

The interesting aspect of this word is the way it is used by the Indonesian people in their daily lives.

Basically, cocok is used instead of good or bad, right or wrong. In other words, an Indonesian person will always tend not to say »right« or »good,« but to use the word »cocok« (suitable) because of the deep belief that something that is good for one person at a particular time can very well be bad for another, and something that is right in a certain culture or tradition can be considered wrong in another place. The word suggests avoiding the dualistic juxtaposition between right or wrong, good or bad, rational and irrational, because on a macrocosmic level, everything has its place.

From a more spiritual and cosmological point of view, the use and choice of the word cocok, while not conscious, is part of a different level of awareness where we learn and practice avoiding judgments, not so much because judging is wrong or bad in itself, but more because »how do I know?« And indeed we know little about the reasons, the motivations, the causes that are behind a certain way of being, acting, feeling, or thinking of someone. We don't know, because we see very little of the full picture.

To sum it up and put it simply, we may say that this word can apply to almost anything: a food can be cocok or not, so could a hat, a place, a weather, a color, a person, an opinion, an idea, a plan, a house, a husband, or a wife. To develop a higher and heightened awareness, cocok is indeed a precious word, and it would be good to use it as often as possible as an alternative to right and wrong. Using it gets us beyond only and always thinking and behaving according to our concepts and judgments separate from the other, and rather learning and practicing being open to the idea that, as an old Javanese saying goes, »That which is good is not necessarily right; that which is right is not necessarily true; that which is true is not necessarily appropriate; that which is appropriate is not necessarily real.«

A word like this could help bring us toward peace, tolerance, acceptance, and yes, cocok would be very cocok in these times of conflict and confusion.

1 *Cocok* ① similar, identical, in accord, compatible; to agree, tally, jibe. *Keterangan Pemerintah – dengan keadaan, yang sebenarnya*. The government's Statement (of Policy) is in accord with the real situation. *Pendapat saudara – dengan pendapat saya*. Your opinion is similar to mine. ② correct, right, precise, exact, fitting. *Arloji saya tidak –*. My watch doesn't keep good time. ③ to appeal strongly to, be to one's taste, suit. *Kalau –, boléh anda beli*. If you like it, you can buy it. ④ to be effective, have an effect, produce the desired results (as of medicine, etc.). *Obat ini sudah diminumnya, tetapi tidak –*. He has already taken this medicine, but it has had no effect. ⑤ to agree, have an un derstanding between/among. *Kita semua – untuk mengemuka- kan keberatan kepada yang berwajib*. There is an understanding among all of us to propose the objections to the proper authorities. ⑥ to fit, be suited, suitable, serve/fulfill the purpose, lend itself to the purpose, go well (with s.t.). *Perkataannya – de- ngan perbuatannya.* His words fit his deeds. *Kunci ini – dengan lemariku.* This key fits my cupboard. *Tanah itu – tidak untuk tanaman tembakau*. The soil is not suitable for growing to bacco. *Rumah ini – sekali untuk rumah makan.* This house lends itself very much to a restaurant. ⑦ in proportion (with). *Hadiah sebanyak itu sudah – dengan jasanya.* Such a large gift is in proportion with his services. *– dengan ukuran cita* to come up to. ⑧ to come true. *Ramalannya –*. His prediction came true. ⑨ to get along well (of people)

Alan M. Stevens and A. Ed. Schmidgall-Tellings Stevens: *A comprehensive Indonesian-English dictionary*, Athens, Ohio 2010.

Filotimo
Filotimo
Filotimo
Filotimo
Filotimo
Filotimo
Filotimo
Filotimo
Filotimo

Filotimo
Philotimo
Φιλότιμο
Alkistis Thomidou

Etymology: From φῐ́λος (phílos = friend, here »loving«) + τῖμή (tīmḗ = honor) + -o (-o)

The most untranslatable, sophisticated, and truly mysterious word in the Greek language is the noun *filotimo*, literally translating into »friend of honor.«[1]

However, filotimo is infinitely more. It is a complex constellation of values that is hard to define; even Greeks cannot agree on one meaning. It describes an array of virtues, including ideas such as honor, justice, dignity, pride, self-sacrifice, respect, gratitude, and hospitality. The core concept is that of small, random acts of kindness that reflect one's personality and the manner in which one was raised. Filotimo describes an attitude toward fellow humans and humanity at large. It means showing empathy, compassion, and generosity without expecting anything in return, taking pride in doing what is right and honorable and being humble at the same time. It extends to appreciation for one's heritage, manifested in love for family, community, and country. Filotimo is something that has to be inspired and cannot be imposed. If one »doesn't have filotimo,« one embarrasses not only oneself but also one's family and community. This idea of being accountable for your family and community pervades Greek culture and makes filotimo, next to *filoxenia* (hospitality), one of the horizontal measures that govern the Greek collective soul. To a Greek, filotimo is essentially a way of life.

Filotimo comes from the word *filotimia*.[2] The first attested written reference of the word dates to the early writings of the Greek Classical period.[3] At that time, filotimia was used in a rather ironic or negative manner, meaning »covetous of honour and distinction,« while the verb *filotimeomai* was used in the sense of »lavish upon.«[4] It took a couple of centuries for the word to gain a positive connotation. Around the fourth and fifth centuries B.C. the meaning shifted from the individual toward the collective, when classical Athens saw the consolidation of democracy, competition was replaced by cooperation, and a man with filotimo was someone who loved to receive the praises of his city but first served the community. From then on it developed in its more noble senses such as meekness, humility, and selflessness. Over the centuries, it was reduced to its modern use, which is infused in all layers of modern Greek society and popular culture,[5] allowing individuals to claim it and give it those different meanings, filling them with pride and confidence.[6]

Peoples and languages invent words out of the necessity to express specific concepts[7] and apparently Hellenism had this need. But where did this need come from; what circumstances promoted its establishment as one of the building blocks of the Greek disposition and imaginary, and why is it relevant today?

In the fifteenth century, while the West was experiencing Enlightenment and developing modern states that tied together individuals under the rule of law and an abstract sense of responsibility, Greece spent 400 years under Ottoman rule, which forced a large part of the population into subsistence farming through heavy taxation and limited education. The subjugated and inward-looking Greeks were bound by pride, localism, and interpersonal relationships. Instead of developing the kind of institutional consciousness seen in Western Europe, Greek communities were imbued with filotimo, which was triggered not by law and logic, but intense emotion and some degree of intimacy.[8]

Those ideas of empathy and intimacy reflect the emotional side to a national character and are the pillars on which the word filotimo is well-founded. They can be found in actions and stories throughout modern Greek history until the most recent days. Decades of poor governance and corruption, the great depression that the ongoing financial crisis caused, followed by a humanitarian crisis and – with a general fear of the Other – the rise of nationalism, exhausted large parts of Greek society. However, people rallied around each other and society kept its cohesion, individuals were mobilized and did their »duty« in solidarity. Solidarity manifests itself through different forms of human values, behaviors, protocols, and negotiations. Filotimo is this common value, the common imaginary, that has kept the Greek community strong and vibrant in the hardest of times.

At the height of the refugee crisis, locals on the eastern Aegean islands[9] dove in icy waters trying to help refugees as their rickety boats reached the shores. Hundreds of fishermen, volunteers, housewives, retirees, teachers, artists, and students waited by the beach every day to offer help and open their homes to people fleeing war and terror – an international disaster in the hands of individuals practicing filotimo. For them it is simply a way of being, and the emotional and moral satisfaction far outweighs any attempt at conceptualizing it. This willingness to open one's home and embrace others, without implicit expediencies and rewards, is care put into practice. I don't have anything, but you can have it all. It is a kind of altruism, but more extroverted, more open. Unlike other forms of relationships (friendship or love) you cannot transmit filotimo on your own, or say »I have filotimo.« It is the intelligence of the Other that defines

»you have filotimo.« In that sense, the word is active, but only through the perspective of the observer. This existence of a bidirectional relationship is fundamental and important. Filotimo entails mutual recognition, coexistence, and togetherness. Beyond the popular »legend« Greeks like to brag about – that filotimo is something that Greeks are born with and that runs through their veins – for me, filotimo is truly a practice of solidarity and care.

In our individualistic, alienating, capitalistic society of constant competition and striving for growth, where »relationships have been converted to services and commons to commodities,«[10] there is an urgency for collective actions that nurture collectivity, solidarity, and care: »civic – person-to-person and horizontal – responsibility that enables people to be able to conduct, with agility, the full spectrum of the stages and elements of care as an ongoing, interrelational practice [...]«[11]

What if we incorporated the principles of filotimo into the fabric of our societies and let it permeate every aspect of our daily lives? Can this multifaceted word, with its multiple meanings and etymological and syntactic peculiarities, bring meaning back into our broken social systems? There is a certain magic around filotimo and its use can be of benefit both on a personal and collective level, be exemplary for a more solidary and care-ful dealing with each other, living well, and thriving.

1 Here, »lover of honor« like filoxenos (hospitable): »lover of foreigners.«

2 »A strong sense of self-worth and dignity, manifested mainly in one's desire to gain the appreciation of others, in our sensitivity to what others think of us.« Georgios Babiniotis: *Dictionary of the Modern Greek Language*, 5th edition, Athens 2019.

3 Sixth and seventh centuries B.C. The word appears, for example, in Plato's Republic, Book 2, section 347b.

4 *The Online Liddell-Scott-Jones Greek-English Lexicon*, entries 114532–114534 of 119556, http://www.perseus.tufts.edu/hopper/text?doc=Perseus:text:1999.04.0057:alphabetic%20letter=*f:entry%20group=31:entry=filotime/omai (accessed November 26, 2020).

5 In postwar Greece, in a time of massive urbanization and internal migration, the emerging and at the time very popular Greek cinema contributed to forming and disseminating specific images of and for Greek society of the nineteen-fifties until the nineteen-seventies. The word »filotimo« is featured in the titles of at least three Greek films.* All three stories highlight the clash of classes in the major urban centers and describe basic ethics of Greek family and society. Usually poor and uneducated people, coming from rural areas to the urban centers in search for better life, struggle to survive and must compete with a wealthy and well-educated urban class in both private and public life. My suggestion is that filotimo in this case was used as a means of empowerment. Here the word takes a more popular meaning, that one might not have wealth and higher education, but rather a big heart and morals. *Λατέρνα, Φτώχεια Και Φιλότιμο (1955) (Laterna, Poverty and Philotimo), Υπάρχει και φιλότιμο (1965) (There is Filotimo, Indeed), Ο Ρωμιός έχει φιλότιμο (1968) (The Greek has Filotimo).

6 It is fair and worthwhile to mention that in Greek popular culture, filotimo has often been used/abused. It has also been cut and sewn, in an opportunistic manner, to fit weaknesses or strengths of different aspects and habits of Greek society, usually connected with national pride, political give and take, and the promotion of personal interests.

7 Philotimo Foundation: Nikos Lygeros talks about filotimo. YouTube video, 13:41, uploaded by Philotimo Foundation, https://www.youtube.com/watch?v=HNVFUf7vw94&ab_channel=PhilotimoFoundation (accessed November 26, 2020).

8 Stav Dimitropoulos. »The Greek word that can't be translated,« in: *BBC Travel*, June 7, 2017, http://www.bbc.com/travel/story/20170605-the-greek-word-that-cant-be-translated (accessed November 26, 2020).

9 Lesbos, Chios, and Kos are well-known tourist destinations that the recession greatly affected.

10 Phineas Harper: »Enough: The Architecture of Regrowth,« in *Dezeen*, September 19, 2017, https://www.dezeen.com/2019/09/25/oslo-architecture-triennale-architecture-degrowth-phineas-harper/ (accessed November 26, 2020).

11 Genevieve Costello: »On Care and Vulnerability,« in: *Solitude Journal, Collective Care & Response-ability*, July 23, 2020, https://www.akademie-solitude.de/de/solitude-journal/on-care-and-vulnerability/ (accessed November 26, 2020).

Gostopriemstvo
Gostopriemstvo
Gostopriemstvo
Gostopriemstvo
Gostopriemstvo
Gostopriemstvo
Gostopriemstvo
Gostopriemstvo
Gostopriemstvo
Gostopriemstvo
Gostopriemstvo

Gostopriemstvo
Остоприемство
(Home Residency)

Alexander Manuiloff

Gostopriemstvo is the word for »hospitality« in Bulgarian and other Slavic languages. In contrast to the German term *Gastfreundschaft*, which is composed of roots meaning »guest« and »friendliness,« gostropriemstvo's elements relate to »guest« and »acceptance.« Without speculating on any differences in the real expression of hospitality between cultures, the German-speaking West linguistically chose to denote the phenomenon more or less as »being friendly to the guest/stranger,« while the Slavic East chose to look at it as »accepting the guest/stranger.«

Accepting or welcoming the stranger into your own environment and circles is a specific relation and it does not entirely coincide in meaning and practice with being friendly. The language gives no concrete answers; it merely opens the door to observing reality from a specific angle. In the current situation of rising nationalism and xenophobia around the globe, the problem of how to really »accept« the stranger/guest is of significant importance. For Bulgarians, one strong cultural implication of gostropriemstvo – which is not obvious from the word alone – is how much it is bound to the idea of »home.« Gostropriemstvo starts at home, and is shown first and foremost at home. The idea that one could invite guests and pay for them to stay at a hotel, for example, is so foreign to southeastern Europeans that it borders on being ridiculous. If you want guests, you invite them to your home.

The cultural practice of »home residency« could be better understood in this context. Why is it possible at all and why here, in Sofia, Bulgaria, and not so much in other places on the map? This interesting trend is still nascent and fragile in my country, but also growing and gaining support.

I am referring to *micro-spaces*, usually operating in privately owned or rented premises no larger than an apartment. These small players are carrying out cultural activities that until recently were the domain of only huge and powerful institutions. The micro-agents are organizing exhibitions, performances, even festivals. They also manage to orchestrate open calls for grants for other artists and provide residencies to foreign artists, writers, dancers, etc., often covering their travel, accommodation, and in some cases even awarding scholarships. Most importantly, these residencies take place in private homes and are usually artist-run. They put their guests directly into the shoes of somebody who lives in the city, the way locals do. The residents do not receive any special treatment – in the sense that they don't get better living conditions or anything that is not usually available to local artists.

Of course, such an approach allows for a more intimate host-artist encounter. But what is also interesting in this home-run situation is that these small agents can now take a portion of public resources and redistribute it to more alternative forms of creation – on a micro-level, of course, which otherwise often, not to say always, remains neglected by state-funding schemes. These »homemade« players can attract and work with artists who would remain outside of the scope of the state vision.

Home residencies are in a way the younger relatives of the 1960s and 1970s artists' squads in Europe, at least in terms of the free spirit they want to somehow keep. The micro-spaces usually want to cut through red tape and officialdom and try to let things happen more naturally. Their activities and projects often instill a sense of community and adopt a more democratic approach to the decision-making process. Unlike the artist squads, however, they are legally registered. They pay for the places they use and can offer better living and working conditions to their guests, still preserving the atmosphere of a »home,« the idea of a place that is prepared for you by friends, not by chambermaids.

Home residencies are also somewhat sustainable. Maintaining these smaller spaces consumes fewer resources, allowing for a less economic-driven approach to the whole organization.

In Bulgaria such spaces are Radar Sofia, Aether, and Swimming Pool. As physical manifestations, none of them are bigger than a normal flat. They are all centrally located and all pay rent. At the same time, they are able to provide their residents with the peace and quiet that is so necessary for creation and reflection. Home residencies can invite guests without necessarily asking them to »produce« something, because they function on a model less driven by output. This approach is something so luxurious that in many cases it has been reserved for and has been the prerogative only of the richest residency programs so far. In Bulgaria, especially, state/municipal support to artists was exclusively reserved for product-oriented projects, and it is exactly the small home players who managed to convince institutions to change their established ways and also give support to guest creators without asking for a tangible final product. This shift of attitude was only possible within a culture in which gostopriemstvo is a legitimate phenomenon.

In an international context, we saw a significant management decision in 2019, when Akademie Schloss Solitude wanted to build a network of exchange residencies in Eastern Europe. Of all the options in Bulgaria, they chose to work precisely with these micro-spaces. This is an important sign that these relatively new and tiny players can provide flexibility and content that is culturally quite specific, and therefore valued.

In 2020 home residencies are now part of the game in Sofia. And this development was to an extent possible due to the mere existence of the word gostopriemstvo, and the way both the language and the cultural tradition have opted to view this phenomenon over the centuries.

Gurukulam

Gurukulam
Gurukulam
Gurukulam
Gurukulam
Gurukulam
Gurukulam
Gurukulam
Gurukulam
Gurukulam

Gurukulam
Prasanna Oommen

When world-class British-Bengali dancer Akram Khan describes in a cinematic portrait how he didn't feel at home until he had children, I prick up my ears. This isn't just because of the by now all too familiar rootlessness of an immigrant child, attested to so often, but instead because this frequent phenomenon is the precise reason I suggested some months ago that we include the word *Gurukulam* in this lexicon.

For the wonderful thing about in situ training in the arts in India is that we, the homeless postmigrants in particular, can find this home in the Gurukulam, in the »house of our Guru,« between the worlds of our parents and the descendants of Western colonial society.[1] In the ideal case, which I was fortunate enough to experience, the teachers there are more than mediators. They can be artistic mentors, life guides, role models, parents, siblings, or grandparents in a world characterized by an initially encoded didactic framework, but which, over time, develops an openness that is second to none. I only fully understood this in retrospect, when my gurus had long since passed.

A brief retrospective: After completing secondary education in Germany and studies in classical Indian dance, which I began when I was five years old, I had the privilege of embarking on an apprenticeship with two elderly master dancers, a married couple from Bangalore, in their school *Maha Maya* (an expression of divine worship that transcends human understanding).[2] The next decade proved an unexpected revelation, not only for me, but for each of my visitors from Germany.

Gurukulam is much more than the mere enjoyment of a high-quality artistic training opportunity. Gurukulam means that the teachers are tasked with promoting the personal development of students through art. Indeed, it is »arts education« at its best, an experience that has had a lasting impact on my subsequent approach to life. My gurus treated us students with an esteem and respect that I had never before encountered from my ballet teacher, the theater director I worked under as a member of a collective theater troupe, or even from my German teachers. A respectful rigor was paired with consummate recognition and encouragement for my unconditional will to learn. However, the aching bones caused by day upon day of training sessions and the demanding theory lessons alone did not make them my gurus. It was far more than that. They welcomed me into their home, their kitchen, their family, their way of life, their values, and their artistic circles, as well as smoothing my path with the other students. In this way, they were the people who facilitated what became, for me, an authentic, holistic relationship with India, giving me access to a truly broad sphere of artistic practice.

The fact that I still find excessively neoliberal promotional practices too attached to funnel thinking and the promotion of elites unreasonable is a direct result of this experience. My convictions were also shaped by the former chemistry professor U. S. Krishna Rao, who was born in 1912 and held a scholarship at the University of Heidelberg in the nineteen-fifties. They are connected to the fact that, despite this great opportunity, he felt called to revive and carry into the world that piece of India's cultural heritage, the 2,000 year-old classical Indian temple dance, which had been banned by the British for 300 years, thus abandoning his scientific career. Of course, they were also shaped by his wife, Chandrabhaga Devi and his granddaughter Anjali, my other teachers, who were and remain the most emancipated women in a traditional society I have ever met. My current beliefs were impacted by my great gurus, who shared their pain about the caste

Prasanna Oommen, Danceschool »Maha Maya«,
Bangalore, 1999, photo: Olaf Hirschberg
Courtesy of the photographer

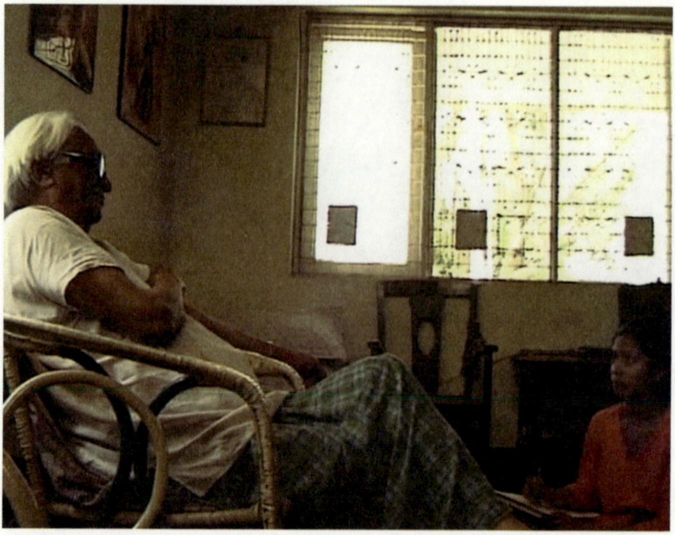

Prasanna Oommen with her teacher Prof. U.S. Krishna Rao, Danceschool »Maha Maya« Bangalore, 1999, photo: Olaf Hirschberg Courtesy of the photographer

system with us because their own guru, the unforgotten Meenakshi Sundaram Pillai, always refused to eat with them because of his origins in a lower caste, as it did not seem appropriate to him. This, despite the fact that they lived under his roof and trained with him until the point of exhaustion.

To me, Gurukulam signifies the following: Learning about this cultural heritage as an equal, as well as the trust that was placed in us thanks to the unwavering power that dance, music, philosophy, and practice was accorded in this household. It stands for unconditional trust in and tolerance for the students, as well as for the knowledge that the core of this art form can only survive and thrive if the new generation is treated well. Because it is never static and reproducible. I remain convinced that my teachers' love of dance has nourished their love for us and their many dozen students worldwide, regardless of religion, origin, class, or gender. It was never important to them that we achieve their particular brand of excellence. Instead, they wanted us to closely study our own incarnation in the artistic process, especially in terms of our gender roles, whose ever-changing demands they sensitively observed. Moreover, the form of Gurukulam in which I was privileged to participate and which can be found with all the great master teachers as well as in contemporary academies in India, was never bound to *one* exclusive discipline or *one* professional career.

Instead, my gurus never tired of encouraging me to complete my studies in Cologne, because they assessed the few opportunities offered to artists from a nonwestern context in a realistic manner. They were privileged Indians familiar with the workings of the colonial system; they knew the mechanisms well, and they countered them with a strong sense of particularly Indian self-confidence that I had not yet experienced in the West. What has Gurukulam taught me personally? A great deal of solidarity with women. To understand discipline and perseverance as a virtue and not as a means of usurping others. To take responsibility within a community, although I was trained solo. The central demand of my gurus was that I should contextualize the knowledge I acquired with my artistic knowledge from the western hemisphere. It follows that this was the precise opposite of an origin-specific cultivation of identity, namely a transcultural and interdisciplinary system, highly modern and absolutely democratic in its roots. Ultimately, a good Gurukulam has an impact on society as a whole, because it accords responsibility to the artists' own personalities. I will conclude this rather different encyclopedia entry thus: *You become a guru on the basis of the sum of the life you have lived. Disciples can grow in the house of such a guru.*

1 Gurukulam means »house of the guru« or »family of the guru.« The term originally comes from the Sanskrit, from »guru« (teacher or master) and »kula« (family or home) and refers to a traditional Indian teaching method in which the students live in the teacher's house, receiving not only subject-related instruction (crafts, sciences, singing, dance, yoga, and so forth), but also help with chores and learn from the guru. The origins of this method go back to 5000 B.C., making it one of the earliest forms of public school. The students live in the Gurukulam, far away from their families of origin, for an extended period. The guru thus becomes a parent and another form of family is created.

2 Important training centers for dance in the Gurukulam tradition include *Nrityagram*, India's first modern Gurukul for classical Indian dances. Founded in 1990 by the Odissi dancer Protima Gauri (previously Protima Bedi, a glamorous, rebelious figure, former model, disco owner and go-go dancer), students study eight hours a day, six days a week for seven years following the ancient Guru-shishya tradition *Kalakshetra*. The Kalakshetra Foundation is a cultural academy for the preservation of traditional Indian arts, particularly music and dance. It combines the Gurukulam system with modern teaching methods and regular examinations as is the case during conventional training. Students learn not only dance, but also music and other related subjects; *Kalamandalam*, in Kerala, also adapted to the regular academic system, combining Gurukulam and modern pedagogy.

Innigkeit
Innigkeit
Innigkeit
Innigkeit
Innigkeit
Innigkeit
Innigkeit
Innigkeit
Innigkeit
Innigkeit

Innigkeit

Regina Dürig
Patrizia Bach

Innigkeit is not a cultural practice, yet. But we would be more than happy to live in a society or community in which Innigkeit guides and shapes our interaction; our way of being ourselves and being with each other. Innigkeit as a way of tender appreciation, of unquestionably acknowledging the other as Other, and quietly embracing their existence as a whole.

Innigkeit, following the seminal German-language dictionary of the Brothers Grimm, has three meanings: the innermost constitution of a human character, a meditation or prayer, or, in more contemporary terms, a deep sentiment.[1] Johann Wolfgang von Goethe is quoted to account for the latter definition. As he writes in *Wilhelm Meisters Lehrjahre* (Wilhelm Meister's Apprenticeship):

> Wie will der Weltmann bei seinem zerstreuten Leben die Innigkeit erhalten, in der ein Künstler bleiben muss, wenn er etwas Vollkommenes hervorzubringen denkt.[2]

So there's a cosmopolitan (back in the day a man of the world) who has a scattered or absentminded life and thus cannot hold fast to the kind of Innigkeit in which an artist has to envelop themselves in order to create something absolute. I am not with Wilhelm Meister here – I guess you just cringed, too – about the creation of perfection as what the artist strives for, but we can leave this irritation aside and instead have a look at Innigkeit here: it thwarts an unfocused state of mind; it is something to be or dwell or be encapsulated in; it implies seeing the state of world rather than covering distances on its surface.

1 Jacob und Wilhelm Grimm: »Innigkeit,« in: *Deutsches Wörterbuch* http://woerterbuchnetz.de/cgi-bin/WBNetz/wbgui_py?sigle=DWB&mode=Vernetzung&lemid=GI00520#XGI00520 (accessed September 30, 2020).

2 Johann Wolfgang von Goethe, *Wilhelm Meisters Lehrjahre*, in: Goethes Werke. Hamburger Ausgabe in 14 Bänden. Band 7. Hamburg 1948, pp. 209–16 http://www.zeno.org/Literatur/M/Goethe,+Johann+Wolfgang/Romane/Wilhelm+Meisters+Lehrjahre/Viertes+Buch/Zweites+Kapitel (accessed September 30, 2020).

Innigkeit is a sentiment, but to me it has an important notion that luminaries Grimm and Goethe hid behind knee-deep pomp or didn't think or know of at the time: a point-blank naïveté, an unconditional and welcoming openness. The best way to describe Innigkeit is to think of yourself in a house with a child or children and remember how they run up to you in the morning after you haven't seen them in a long time, how they hug your legs with their arms and compact hands, how you bend down to embrace them and smell their hair, how they close their eyes, and you, for a moment, do too. This moment of two presences being connected, not through necessity but admiration or care or wonder alone, is the essence of Innigkeit.

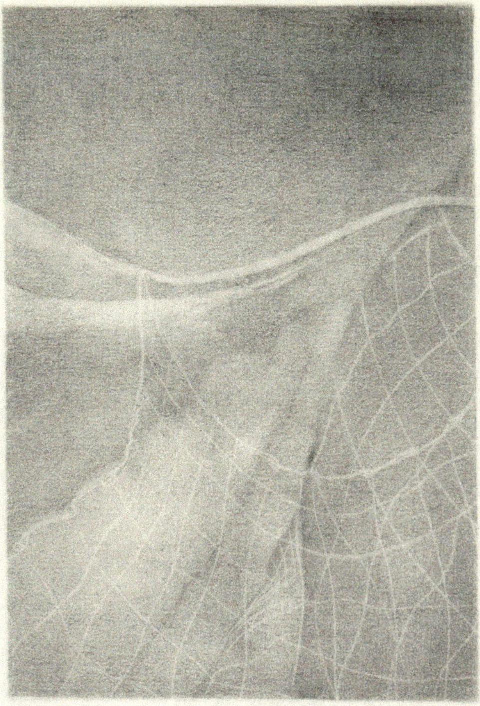

The above child is not coincidental – to love someone *innig* (dearly) is a phrase that you would say about a kid (*she loves her teacher innig*) and not about an adult (or only metaphorically – *my husband loves his coffee-maker innig*). Innigkeit is a questionless and unquestionable practice of gentleness and enthusiasm that, like so many others, kids seem to instinctively know, whereas the grownups have to be reminded, mindful about.

Innigkeit can also be practiced in reading. I infinitely enjoy the one breath in which my eyes are closed and somebody else's words embrace my body's warmth. Like this, I read Ludwig Wittgenstein or Martin Heidegger or Helène Cixous or Luce Irigaray. I cannot own or control; I cannot manipulate or master. All I can do is be present, holding up my end of the text, leaning carefully in. It was in such circumstances that, to my surprise, I found that Innigkeit cannot be translated to English, at least not in one word. I read Heidegger's essay »Language« first in German and later in the English translation. And this is what I was told: »For world and things do not subsist alongside one another. They penetrate each other. Thus the two traverse a middle. In it, they are at one. Thus at one they are intimate. The middle of the two is intimacy.« [3] But in Heidegger's original, the »middle of the two« is not »intimacy.« The middle of the two is Innigkeit: nothing carnal or sexual, nothing that needs to be awkwardly shown or carefully hidden or joyfully talked about, nothing that potentially conjugates distance or silently points into difference. Maybe Innigkeit is intimacy, but minus all the physical awkwardness that may or may not occur.

3 Martin Heidegger: *Poetry, Language, Thought*. New York 2001: p. 199.

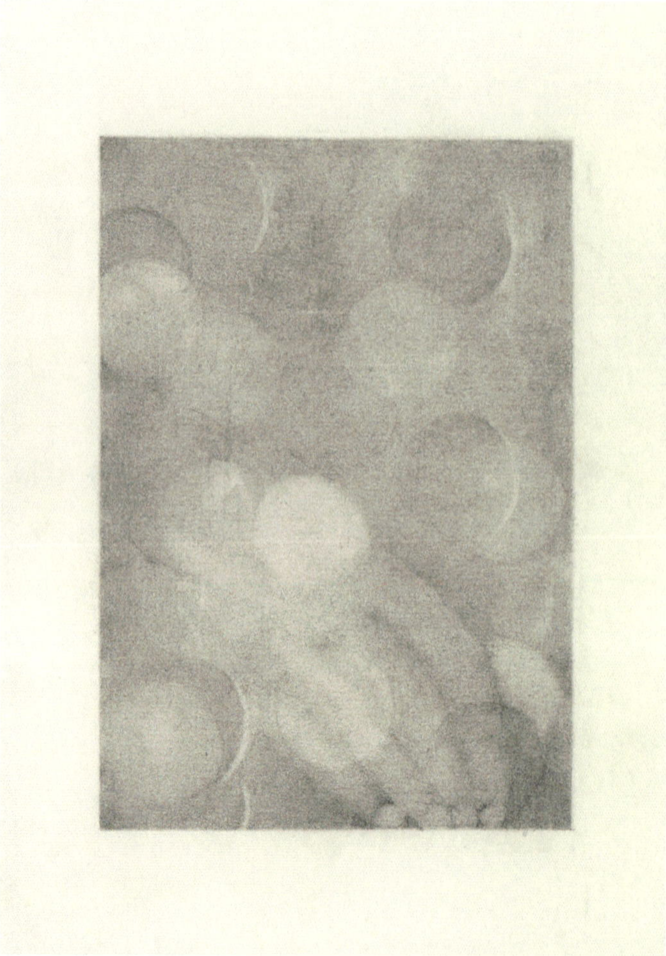

Apropos awkwardness – the English version of the Goethe quote. I know that most attempts at definition fall flat, which to me is a true relief because it means that drawing lines and borders is more nonsensical than we can ever imagine. But in the official 1885 translation of *Wilhelm Meister*, the absence of sense is quite spectacular. There seems to have been a veritable Innigkeits-struggle, a linguistic exertion which called for, quite mystically, the appearance of a *special object*: »And after all, how shall a fashionable man of the world, with his dissipated habits, attain that intimate presence with a special object, which an artist must long continue in, if he would produce anything approaching to perfection?«[4]

The special object – a strongbox, a blanket, a fountain pen. Iron or wool or ivory. An object to make sure that body wasn't meant? A necklace, a heavy coat, a midnight blue carpet. How would one achieve an intimate presence with an object anyway? The object appears as counteragent for the genuine ability to be gently present. A presence without calculation or trade-off maybe even without consequence.

4 Johann Wolfgang von Goethe: *Goethe's Works, vol. 4 (Recreations of the German Emigrants, Wilhelm Meister's Apprenticeship)*, 1885; https://oll.libertyfund.org/titles/2274#Goethe_0841-04_1460 (accessed September 30, 2020).

In an economy of Innigkeit, the currency would be presence without denomination. In a world that is built on welcoming the other in a silent embrace, we would have enough time to find words to say to each other and about ourselves without the fear of being confused with an object whatsoever. It would be a world, perhaps, a world and a writing »in which we don't manufacture word-objects, cans, jewel boxes, ›books.‹ We create paths, in movements.«[5]

Text: Regina Dürig
Drawings: Patrizia Bach, 20 × 14 cm, pencil on paper, 2020
Courtesy of the artist

5 Helène Cixous: *Weiblichkeit in der Schrift*, Berlin 1980: p. 20. Translation by the author.

Juogi
Juogi
Juogi
Juogi
Juogi
Juogi
Juogi
Juogi

Juogi

Enos Nyamor

Illustration by ZZDD
Courtesy of the artist

Psychology, as a scientific study of the human mind and an attempt to demystify behavioral patterns, is essentially an offshoot of Western thought. Through psychoanalytic systems, for example, psychology aims at configuring variations in personality, but as an outcome of an individual's interaction with the immediate surroundings, as well as a clash between conscious and unconscious elements in the mind. But this conceptualization of behavior and personality, set within the limits of pragmaticism and scientific methods, fails to capture the essence of psychic energy that is attached to the supernatural, and which the Luo of East Africa define as *juogi*.

Juogi encapsulates the connection between the world of the living and that of the spirits – of non-human consciousness. Among the Luo, non-human consciousness is elevated above the objective reality of human experience. Even the common mode of meaning/making in the Luo language, deeply embedded in semiotics, denotes a relationship between everyday life and non-human beings. Thus, in the value system, the human body, although considered whole, is first divided into autonomous organs. These organs are in turn susceptible to invasion by outside forces that roam the earth. And above all, these organs can also embody an agency, and can act contrary to personal resolve – in opposition to one's firm mental determination.

When, for instance, one experiences a stomach ache, the literal interpretation in English would be that »one's belly is biting.« The stomach is granted a form of unwarranted aggression. The conceptualization of the outside forces also extends to aspects of human life such as sleep and the ultimate reality that is death. Sleep is in itself a creature that can pounce on one, and when a person is on the verge of going to bed, instead of deploying the phrase »feeling sleepy,« might say »sleep has defeated me.« Likewise, death, too, is a force that can be avoided and can either be natural or unnatural. It is an agent that takes away life, but also coordinates with one's juogi.

Juogi, then, is life in a different form trapped outside of oneself, but which oversees one's interactions with nature and society. It is part of a vast network of non-human beings, influenced by the supernatural, yet unique to each person. And although unique to every individual, one can embody a multiplicity of these non-human forces, and so that accounts for the term juogi, which is plural. But this term is often carefully applied, especially in relation to a more sinister *juok*, which is referenced in the singular. Those with only the juok are considered diabolical, meaning that there is an absence of a dialectic among one's personal spirits, and this uniformity can result into deviant behaviors. Those who commit acts of transgression are considered to embody juok and not juogi, for their actions are judged unnatural.

The distinction between the term juogi and the term personality, which is the closest translation in English, is that it applies to different contexts in daily life. Although empiricism is the pedestal upon which the modern understanding of personality thrives, the existing methods still discount the mysteries of nature. To understand the significance of the term juogi, however, requires an unsurmountable recognition of motivations beyond one's limited life experience. Juogi, as such, is attached to a form of atemporality – existing outside the human conception of time – as this denotes both reincarnation and a continuing growth process.

And so, one's behavioral pattern under the lens of juogi is eternally connected to the behavior of those who preceded one, such as grandparents or the person one is named after. It is for this reason that the Luo have a tradition of naming children after heroes. When a child is born days after a prominent member of a community dies, the parents would opt to name the child after the hero, with the hope that the child would absorb some of the greatness. It often happens that many children in the same community are named after the same legend, making it possible to deduce the generation to which a person belongs.

But the essence of the term is not only to aspire to reincarnation, especially of celebrated personalities, but to also enhance harmony within a community, in which case juogi is applied in the context of idiosyncrasy. In Luo customs, the community or the clan occupies a central position in the shaping of an individual's identity. It is essential that the community or parents observe the child in their formative years and begin to develop an understanding of their character traits. There are those children whose behaviors are commonplace and predictable, but there are those who exhibit peculiarities, and these are the ones considered to embody juogi. Those with juogi primarily demonstrate constant mood swings. Even as adults, whenever such individuals display an unconventional attitude, it behooves those around to respond amicably, in order to assuage their spirits.

While juogi is applied in identifying those with volatile personality, and setting context for social harmony, it is also a term that is subjectively applied to oneself. It is a form of configuring one's emotional chaos. When a person is thrust into a mood swing, then it is apparent that one's juogi has deserted them. The remedy to such a crisis often involves a series of rituals, until a restoration of emotional, mental, and spiritual harmony is achieved. Such an obsession is not considered as a disorder that demands clinical interventions, for example, but as a way in which a person relates to their overbearing juogi.

No doubt this term is instrumental in fostering social harmony and in configuring both mental and emotional state. But it is widely applied to those gifted with special abilities. Juogi encapsulates moods, personality, idiosyncrasy, and also talents. Artistic gifts are affiliated with juogi, and, almost without exception, all artists are bundled together because of their unconventional lifestyles. It is one way that the Luo criticize a work of art, based on the capacity of the artist to induce the juogi in the audience – to transport the audience beyond its objective reality. All musicians and storytellers, for that matter, are considered to be naturally endowed with juogi, for this is the source of their inspiration and what instructs them in their creative processes. When placed in context, an artist residency like Akademie Schloss Solitude would not only be a space for creatives, but also a place occupied by those possessing, or possessed by, juogi.

Langar
Langar
Langar
Langar
Langar
Langar
Langar
Langar
Langar

Langar

Simar Preet Kaur

The six-letter noun *langar* is understood as »an open kitchen in a Gurdwara run by the Sikh community.« That makes it eleven words, and yet they lack the intent that drives the 500-year-old practice of serving free meals to everyone. Let's try a different translation.

Langar's linguistic roots are uncertain. Some trace the word to Sanskrit, others to Persian. But for all practical purposes, it is a Punjabi concept that originated in the sixteenth century in the now-irretrievably divided north-western parts of the Indian subcontinent. It was a fractured land back then, too; subject to conquerors' whims and governed by the self-righteous. Langar was – is – an attempt to undo those redundant distances that continue to separate us from each other.

Langar has a historical context. It is attributed to Guru Nanak Dev, the saint upon whose teachings Sikhism was founded, and his successors who institutionalized it. Sikhism is currently the world's fifth-largest organized religion, but it's also the youngest, and it really began as a spiritual movement away from the existing web of social taboos – a simplification of rituals and a shift from sprawling iconography to a more tangible core. Amongst its basic tenets is the practice of contributing ten percent of one's time or earnings to the community. Langar, in this case, is a manifestation of that return to the collective; it remains as relevant today: a symbolic act of sitting on equal ground to partake of a meal, regardless of one's religion, caste, class, gender, and ethnicity.

When first established, langar was a revolutionary act that disregarded discrimination in all its forms. An unusual religious tradition that challenged religious exclusivity. Langar, then, can be interpreted as a humanitarian gesture built on the essentials without which no life, however evolved, can survive – food and water.

But langar doesn't conclude with a lofty definition; it is also a commitment that has acquired the scope of large-scale operations. Every *Gurdwara* – the place of worship for Sikhs – has a mandatory Langar Hall and kitchen on its premises. What sets it apart from food banks or soup kitchens is the encouragement of dual participation, through reception and service. Anyone interested in contributing to the preparation and serving of such meals is welcomed; the Langar Hall and kitchen are places where selflessness is propagated through a daily virtue known as *Seva*. On ground, it means organizing meals for thousands within the span of a few hours. An adaptable practice, because if those thousands in need are unable to make it to the dining hall, langar goes out to them.

When extrapolated from the point of view of recent world events, langar translates as a philosophy of solidarity. The Sikh community has been at the forefront organizing food and shelter for the vulnerable during the darkest hours – feeding refugees in Bangladesh and Syria, flood victims in Kerala, Kashmiri students forced into evacuation, riot victims in the Delhi violence against Muslims, CAA protestors at Shaheen Bagh and Black Lives Matter protestors in New York; reaching out with food to firefighters battling the Australian bushfires and those left homeless in their midst; distributing cooked meals and food rations during the pandemic in the worst-affected corners of the world – to stranded migrant workers, hospital staff, exhausted policemen, and the underprivileged, but also to just about anyone who's hungry. »Hunger,« for that matter, is also an unusual word. It has no appropriate synonyms and yet every living thing on earth apprehends its physicality.

Langar arouses suspicion on first encounter. Free? For what? A reflection of our state of global mistrust. But it's simple stuff. Hygienic vegetarian meals funded by donations and served by volunteers. The whole thing operates on mutual trust. No proselytizing, no judgments, no expectations. At the doors of a Langar Hall, you trade your ego and footwear for compassion and humility. Call it »charity« during good times. Or »relief« during natural disasters, and during the harshest of them all, man-made tragedies. The practice of serving and eating cuts across religions; it isn't what makes Sikhism ontologically unique. What is worth emulating is the way in which langar has managed to embed itself with grace and without much fuss in many political issues as a symbol of hope, without emphasizing the religious aspect.

Given the awkward consequences of individualism in our hands, a vocabulary for a transformative future would have to lean toward practices that address the species as a whole. Words of inclusion that acknowledge our interconnectedness. Is there a way that langar, as a practice of sharing – and daring, especially in these agitated times – can be expanded with its inherent generosity into a more accessible language?

We could articulate it another way. Langar as something elementary. The word has a signature sweetness to it – the taste of cardamom-flavored rice pudding served at the end of the meal. It has a soundscape that extends from the clatter of thousands of steel utensils to the quiet plop of a flatbread, the round roti, into hands unfolded in gratitude. It has a smell, too – that of comfort food cooked in gigantic cauldrons. The largest langar kitchen in the world, located at the Golden Temple in Amritsar, functions round-the-clock and serves up to 150,000 people on a regular day. Here langar is a sight: rows upon rows of strangers, a mix like that of a crossroads, but sitting side by side on the floor. Langar is a noun that hopes to touch and be touched by everyone.

You recall Brecht's famous maxim? »Grub first, then ethics.« This one's more like grub-in-the-name-of-ethics. We share food, then we live to share ideas.

Simple stuff in a neutral space. Sit. We eat together.

A Langar at Singhu – right on the border of Delhi with Haryana – serving dinner to all who feel like eating late on a very cold night. Since 26th of November nearly one hundred thousand farmers – mostly from Punjab and Haryana – have been camping at Singhu when their march to Delhi in protest against the new farm laws the Government introduced was stalled. Sikhs have opened more than a hundred Langars at Singhu to feed protesters and their supporters every day
31.12.2020, photo: Mitra Joydip
Courtesy of the photographer (joydipmitraphotography.com)

Mapalus
Mapalus
Mapalus
Mapalus
Mapalus
Mapalus
Mapalus
Mapalus
Mapalus

Mapalus

Natasha Tontey

For Indonesians, North Sulawesi has always been known for its sea and forest. The Minahasan people are also known for their local eating habits, which are often categorized as bizarre. These eating habits, along with the commodification of game meat[1] including rodents, wild boars, monkeys, bats, even cats and dogs, have made many people question the ethics of Minahasan culture. Many environmentalists and wildlife rescue groups think that eating game should be prohibited. »This tradition is no longer ideal, it causes the loss of biodiversity,«[2] says one conservationist. This opinion perpetuates an assumption that the damage to biodiversity emerges solely from the tradition of the Minahasan indigenous community. However, what is also missing from these assumptions is that eating game indicates a strong relationship between people and the forest, beyond the meat's commodification and marketization. The Minahasan people believe that forests are the source of life, the property of no one. Forests are a common resource. This goes back to the Minahasan philosophy Mapalus, a well-structured tenet of mutual assistance.

Based on a kinship structure, Mapalus is understood as a way of thinking collectively. It is applied to all lines of Minahasan life: relationships and interactions among humans, nonhumans, as well as with ancestors. Technically, Mapalus comes from the Minahasan words *Ma* and *Palus*. Ma is an active verb to indicate an activity, while palus means to fulfill each other, or filling a glass with water. Contextually, the water symbolizes that our activities are complementary and reciprocal; always an act of fulfilling each other. It must be mutual. Reciprocity here is a manifestation of *adat* (customary law).

In an attempt at nation-making, the »founding fathers« of Indonesia constructed something that is understood as Indonesian identity. *Gotong royong* (a term translated as mutual aid or mutual assistance in Indonesian, which is rooted in Malay and Javanese language) is brought forward as a national identity. This term becomes the backbone of what many understand as Indonesian philosophy. However, gotong royong, as a nation-making mantra, is hardly understood by the Minahasan people. Although it seems similar, Mapalus as a system of thinking that is structurally and culturally embodied in the

Minahasa community has a fundamental difference from gotong royong. In practice, Mapalus can indeed reductively be categorized as mutual aid. However, Mapalus as a philosophy of life has its origin as a structured system and mechanism in agricultural life of Minahasa society, therefore the feature of this word is more complex than what Indonesia tries to construct with their umbrella term gotong royong. In this sense, Mapalus can also be understood as a group of people that work collectively for some specific form of labor. For example, the agricultural system in Minahasa is divided into several Mapalus groups; i.e. Mapalus milu (Mapalus corn) and Mapalus beras (Mapalus rice). This group formation occurred because there was a division of resources and labor in agriculture; for example, after the corn harvest, Mapalus milu will work in the paddy fields with the Mapalus beras, and Mapalus beras will also work in the corn field as a mutual action. This is a form of agricultural reciprocity. Therefore, Mapalus is not just a word to explain mutual aid, but also a cultural way to think systematically.

In addition, the principle of solidarity reflected in Mapalus is manifested in the community as well in the economic system of the Minahasa community. This economic principle is also known as *tamber*, especially for Toulour [3] people. Tamber refers to an activity of gift-giving without any expectation of reciprocity. A person will give a gift to others, or *warga sewanua* (village), voluntarily without obligation. Thus, to return to the prejudice toward the Minahasan habit of eating game meat, it needs to be analyzed from this complex relationship with nature according to the Mapalus concept, while at the same time addressing the commodification of cultural activities. Mapalus as a notion of solidarity between humans and non-humans can be applied to globalized knowledge.

1 See Theodora Sutcliffe: »Indonesia's Best – and Goriest – Cuisine,« in: *BBC Culture*, April 20, 2016. Available online at http://www.bbc.com/travel/story/20160419-indonesias-best-and-goriest-cuisine (accessed November 18, 2020).

2 *Eating Snakes, Rats, and Dogs in Minahasa*: Indonesian Bushmeat, YouTube video, 19:44 min., uploaded by *Vice Asia*, October 25, 2019, www.youtube.com/watch?v=iesrnwTzqr4 (accessed November 18, 2020).

3 Interviews with Fendy E.W. Parengkuan, a Minahasan historian and lecturer who works and lives in Tondano (modern name for Toulour) on January 4, 2020, and September 8, 2020. In direct translation, »Toulour« means »water person.« Toulour is one of the nine subethnicities of Minahasa that participated in the stone pact of Watu Pinawetengan.

Micchāmi Dukkadam
Micchāmi Dukkadam
Micchāmi Dukkadam
Micchāmi Dukkadam
Micchāmi Dukkadam
Micchāmi Dukkadam
Micchāmi Dukkadam
Micchāmi Dukkadam
Micchāmi Dukkadam

Micchāmi Dukkaḍaṃ

Nishant Shah

Every year, on the day of Samvatsari, after 24 hours of fasting marking eight days of austerity and introspection, people following Jainism – a small sect in India founded as a protest against Hinduism's abusive and toxic caste-based practices – bow their heads, bring their hands together, and utter Micchāmi Dukkaḍaṃ. Originating in Prakrit, one of the vernacular scripts of Sanskrit, the phrase has been translated in different ways:

> A banishment of wrong:
> »May all evil that has been done be in vain.«
>
> A condemnation of wrongdoing:
> »May all evil actions be inconsequential.«
>
> A forgiveness for causing harm:
> »I ask pardon from all living beings.«

These multiple interpretations of the phrase are all simultaneously valid and co-constitutive. It is a thesis on violence that departs from the smooth binaries of victims-perpetrators, individuals-structures, and instead proposes a trifecta of actions and reflections that we need to consider in our quest for a post-violent future.

In banishing all that is evil and wrong, the phrase necessitates a recognition and dialogue of things that have been wrong. It demands an honest and hard acceptance that there has been evil, that there has been wrongdoing, and that we take an active role in stopping its expansion. It is a commitment to not just accept the state of things – to see them as they are – but also to map our relationality to them. Evil does not have its own autonomous agency; we are deeply implicated in its spread and sustenance.

Hence the condemnation of the consequences of evil actions, where we acknowledge that these actions have tangible harms. These harms are often experienced by those who can least afford to bear them. They are not small, and if left unattended, they can amplify evil. It is urgent to not only stop the evil action, but also to counteract it. Inaction is not an option. Merely not doing evil or harm is not enough to change the course of these wrong deeds.

Thus comes the third ask of forgiveness, which announces that we have been deeply embedded and indifferent to the state of the world for the evil to have arisen in thought and translated into action. The act of forgiveness is to take responsibility that this evil has not been perpetrated outside of our knowledge or without our consent. We might not be directly participating in its actions, but we seek to benefit and often turn a blind eye because we are not directly affected by its unfolding. In accepting responsibility, we also acquire humility: that we might have failed, that we might have tried and not succeeded, that we might not have understood the consequences of these actions, and now is the time to reckon the hurt and deal with its presence in our lives.

These three modes of operation form a profound thesis on violence: It accepts that we perform violence in speech, action, and thought. However, it does not stop at recognizing these spaces and actions of violence. Instead, it makes us aware that our role in shaping a post-violent future is urgent, emergent, and personal. It forces the person making the utterance witness that violence is a part of our life force. It establishes violence not only as a pathology, but also as a significant part of our modes of survival and being, and in that, provides a moment of reflection of the multiple sources, resources, and life forms that go into our own well-being and survival.

In this threefold manifestation, Micchāmi Dukkaḍaṃ presents a worldview that is quite different from the one we know. The pre-wired responses to violence are recognizable. We immediately identify violence as an exceptional moment and isolate it from our everyday walks and ways of life. In doing so, we often sever its connection from underlying causes and principles, and focus almost all our attention on resolving the symptom at hand rather than looking at the context within which it occurs. In a similar vein, an act of violence, or more particularly, a recognizable act of violence, stages familiar patterns of victims, survivors, and perpetrators.

The act of violence is identified as a unified force and often casts the survivor as without agency and even without identity. It reduces the entire spectrum of violence into one act, and in that, both the survivor and the perpetrator become flat icons rather than complex human beings. Violence is met with justice, but as feminist intervention has repeatedly shown, justice is just violence turned on its head, and not necessarily a way outside of violence. Justice is a redirection of violence and without the considerations of care, restoration, and reparation, it escalates the conditions that led to the violence without necessarily diffusing and rearranging it.

Micchāmi Dukkaḍaṃ captures a fundamental transformation of these narratives of violence for our future. By embracing nonviolence as a core principle, it rescues it from being a negative space – a space empty of violence – and instead offers it as a way of engaging in a conversation with our implicit, complicit, covert, and covetous relationships with different forms of violence. It does so by placing the human subject at the center of the dialogue, and by mapping violence as a default force from which we need to actively free ourselves. Additionally, it challenges us to take responsibility to stop as well as protect those adversely affected by violence.

In this utterance and its cultural context of violence in everyday life, it offers a connected future that unflinchingly recognizes the endemic structures of violence that support our lives. In doing so, it no longer seeks violence as a counterforce. It thus moves away from the »extinction impulse« of our response to violence – one where making violence extinct often results in making people extinct. Instead, it proposes an aspirational quest to transform the way we are, so that all things might survive.

Oisiveté Oisiveté Oisiveté Oisiveté Oisiveté Oisiveté Oisiveté Oisiveté Oisiveté Oisiveté

Oisiveté
Jérôme Toussaint

Labor is everywhere!

In post-industrialized societies, a significant part of labor is immaterial, digital, fluid, limited in time, performance-oriented, achievable everywhere.

We – the workforce – are adaptable, flexible, physically and mentally mobile, always reachable, smoothly managed. We are activable human capital.

Besides, we are always soliciting, applying. LinkedIn is our FB. FB is our LinkedIn. We are brands, entrepreneurs of ourselves, assessing the cost/benefit, mentally if not already legally independent entrepreneurs. We kept the bill after having had a drink with you. You enjoyed our company.

Business is everywhere!

We are lying teleworkers stuck in our soft and ultra-connected prisons.[1] The coronavirus has finished off Fordism. Our laptops optimize the extraction of our work.

We are said to be detached, disloyal, opportunistic, and cynical. We are curious, adaptable, disobedient. Stressed and depressed.[2] We forgot how to unplug.

. . .

In recent years, some authors have called for laziness as a resistance mechanism.

But »laziness« is too dubious. It does counterintelligence, always on the side, trying to make you feel guilty.

»Leisure« is acquainted with entertainment.

»Idleness,« like the German *Müßiggang*, is better.

But the French *oisiveté* has the virtue of being rooted in the Latin word *otium*.

Through Müßiggang, Nietzsche only praised the otium.[3]

The Greeks and early Romans clearly distinguished *otium* and *negotium*. The latter being the negation of the first one (nec otium). Otium comes directly from the Greek *skhôlè*, which covers free time, inaction, studious leisure, the quest of beauty, sense, values, truth. It enables thoughts, contemplation, meditation, study, and speculation. It is autonomous, detached from any personal interests, and deployed without any external justification. It is a side of self-care, the *viva contemplativa*. The way to reach art, politics (as the quest of general interest), philosophy. The ontological basis of individual emancipation.[4]

With the rise of the Roman empire, the otium has been progressively locked in the private sphere. In doing business (negotium), Greeks and early Romans were literally negating the otium (nec otium).

Later, in the Christian era, time was counted by God and it was therefore forbidden to waste it. The so-called principle of non-oisiveté.[5] The pastoral power directed the consciences. Self-revelation – which is at the core of the oisiveté – became self-denial.

The Classical age (the seventeenth and eighteenth centuries) posed the principle of a theoretically ever-growing use of time/workforce. The rise of capitalism. Utilitarianism. Disciplines. Efficiency. This is still ongoing.

So, the fact that the French word oisiveté comes from and therefore envelops the otium has to be praised. It is better equipped this way than »laziness,« »leisure,« or even »idleness« to challenge the world trade of things and its corollary, the ever-growing labor market.

Oisiveté is treated by French-speaking people with distance but without disdain. Neither ideologues nor human resource management thinkers like it. The concept has not aged, but does not seem to fit in our time.

Are *oisifs* or *oisives* the ones who do not work, temporarily or durably, who do not have any kind of business or pseudo[6] activity? They are not lazy, no Bartleby. They are not employed – they are birds.[7]

That essential peace in the depths of our being, that priceless absence in which the most delicate elements of life are refreshed and comforted, while the inner creature is in some way cleansed of past and future, of present awareness, of obligations pending and expectations lying in wait ... No cares, no tomorrow, no inner pressure, but a kind of repose in absence, a beneficent emptiness that brings the mind back to its true freedom. Here it is concerned only with itself. Freed from its obligations toward practical knowledge, and unburdened of any care for things to come, it creates forms as pure as crystal.[8]

Paul Valéry, *The outlook for intelligence*

1 See Paul Preciado: »Biosurveillance: sortir de la prison molle de nos intérieurs,« in: *Mediapart*, April 12, 2020.

2 See Paolo Virno: *A Grammar of the Multitude*, Cambridge, MA 2004.

3 See Friedrich Nietzsche: *The Gay Science*, Cambridge 2001. n° 329.

4 See Jean Miguel Pire: *Otium*, Arles 2020.

5 See Michel Foucault: *Surveiller et punir*, Paris 1995.

6 »People intervene all the time, ›do something‹; academics participate in meaningless debates and so on.« Slavoj Žižek: *Violence: Six Sideways Reflections*, London 2009, p. 183.

7 As oisiveté is spread into sounds, French-speaking people first hear *oiseau*, which means bird in French. Oiseau and oisiveté are the only two common French words beginning with »ois-« and the first one is much more used than the second, so that phonologically the bird cannot be clearly separated from oisiveté.

8 See Paul Valéry: *The Outlook for Intelligence*, trans. Denise Folliot and Jackson Mathews, Princeton 1989.

Sahaja
Sahaja
Sahaja
Sahaja
Sahaja
Sahaja
Sahaja
Sahaja
Sahaja
Sahaja

Sahaja

Vipul Rikhi

Simple, spontaneous, easy, natural.

The word *sahaja* is made up of two components. »Saha« means »with« or »together.« And »ja« refers to birth. So the literal meaning would translate as born, or arising, together.

In common parlance or usage, sahaja points to when something is or has become easy, in the best sense: natural, unforced, spontaneous, and without effort. How does the idea of *arising together* correlate with the idea and practice of the simple, the effortless, easy, and natural?

In Indian philosophy, sahaja indicates a state of mind and being and a practice beyond striving for something – in which there is no gap between the word and the deed, the conception and the execution, the vision and the reality, the object and the self. In other words, it indicates a state of no alienation.

In many schools of Indian thought, reality is understood to arise afresh in each individual moment, ever renewing itself in each alive moment of perception. No one moment or circumstance is exactly the same as any previous one. And so, in human terms – in terms of ethics, morality, expression, artistic practice, and everyday behavior – rules, theories, and »replicability« are often unnatural in the sense that they have to be mentally or externally enforced. Sahaja is the opposite of the idea of enforcement.

Bulbul on My Balcony, Goa, India, 2020, photo: Vipul Rikhi
Courtesy of the photographer

This translates directly into action. There is no attempt at force-fitting reality into a preconceived idea. Facts or practices do not need to accommodate themselves to theory. Seeming intellectual contradiction is not a problem, though ethical and/or artistic integrity is always maintained. Each moment, or each artistic or cultural act, calls for its own code of morality or action.

As the nature of fire is to burn, the nature of the tree to grow and give fruit, the nature of water to flow, so is the nature of consciousness to seek expression in various forms. To realize this as part of one's own nature is to become sahaja, or natural. And there is an endless variety of natures, or therefore, of expressions. Sahaja involves being true to oneself in the moment, as well as responding to the demands of each situation. It does not mean »doing as one likes.«

It is not opposed to the idea of »law« or »rules« – instead, it postulates surrender to the law or truth of the moment, which might be different to anything one might have previously imagined. The idea of »truth« is not considered problematic because it does not signify »One Essential / External / Eternal Truth,« but rather the truth of each individual moment, ethical and creative at the same time. It also does not imply, in a postmodern way, that all truths are equal, or equally valid; rather, it insists that being true is the highest value.

In each moment, there is the possibility and the potential for a new reality to arise. The Buddhist doctrine of »co-dependent origination« says that everything in creation depends on everything else. Each moment calls for a fresh response. To be able to recognize the truth of the moment and to be able to act or be accordingly – without a lag or a gap, using the whole of one's knowledge but without bringing prejudices or prior beliefs into the picture – is the ideal of sahaja.

It could be like a skill that one takes hours and hours to master and which, finally, becomes so much part of oneself that it is no longer any effort at all. The difficult becomes simple, the seemingly impossible becomes natural. In that state, one seems spontaneously to know what exactly to do in each moment (of creation), even though one may have never done so before. One stands out of one's own way.

Sahaja is a term of deep resonance in Buddhist philosophy as well as Hindu religious literature as well as traditional Indian art practice. It represents the epitome of the human possibility of being as well as of artistic and cultural expression. It is the place where the ultimate sophistication ends in a startling simplicity. It recognizes and celebrates diversity and yet bases itself on an inner coherence – a necessary formula for fractious times such as ours!

The »no-gap« between idea or inspiration on the one hand, and realization or expression on the other, is to be understood in terms of integrity. This indicates the least amount of loss, or compromise, from the »ideal« to the »real.« And so the artist's practice is related to the artist's state of being. They are not separate. The artist has to cultivate himself or herself as well as his/her* art. Similarly, in daily life, how one acts must be deeply aligned with how one is (and thinks and feels).

Sahaja can be a vital tool for the modern mind to come to a sense of its own roots. While deeply embedded in a traditional ethos, it speaks of a timeless human truth, which can translate into daily living and practice even in our most fragmented of times. It finds its place in this vocabulary as an untranslatable yet deeply relatable paradigm. It is a vision that brings transformation.

Current and future societies will need to find the sahaja in themselves and for themselves. For me, personally, it remains an abiding principle, which signifies free space, full hearts, and a complete alignment of body, mind, and spirit – a healing remedy for our ideologically and politically fractured times!

Saxansaxo
Saxansaxo
Saxansaxo
Saxansaxo
Saxansaxo
Saxansaxo
Saxansaxo
Saxansaxo

Saxansaxo

Faduma Abukar
Abukar Mursal

The word *saxansaxo* describes a meteorological phenomenon that has social and affective implications. It qualifies how the air is felt before the rain; the smell of the first raindrops that smell really good, and how the water makes the sky almost sparkle. When the wind blows smoothly before it brings the first drops of rain, it is a momentary good feeling, making it comfortable to stay outside for that moment of joy.

Before we elaborate on this word, let us mention how to pronounce saxansaxo. The word is Somali, a Cushitic language spoken by more than thirty-five million speakers, especially in the Horn of Africa as well as by Somalis living across the globe. Part of the Afroasiatic family, the language is phonetically close to Arabic. It was principally verbal, and the Latin script was introduced in 1971 for

Heavy rain clouds, 2020, photo: Abukar Mursal
Courtesy of the photographer and Faduma Abukar

written expression.[1] For instance, the letter x in the Somali alphabet corresponds phonetically to the Arabic letter »ح«. So, the word saxansaxo is pronounced »*sahansaho*,« with the h pronounced just as bit lighter than in »he.«

Saxansaxo is a condition that announces the arrival of a heavy rainfall after a long period of dryness and of awaiting relief. The word has been particularly important for the pastoral communities who are entirely nomadic and live in a semi-arid environment. Normally, saxansaxo happens once a year. However, when it doesn't, it is a year of drought, and saxansaxo is expected the following year, or worse, the year after. The pastoralists distinguish the wind characteristic of the saxansaxo moment from other winds, like the usual wind (*dabeel*), the one that occurs in the hot daytime (*xanfaf*), or in the night (*neecaaw*), all of which are rarely followed by much rain. To recognize saxansaxo is to be assured that heavy rain will follow – the wind that characterizes it is different from a wind that only pushes the clouds away or is followed by sporadic rain that dries up in a day or two. As soon as thunder and lightning start, the »saxansaxo moment« has shifted to other places, and it is time to collect and prepare containers to store the rainwater and find shelter.

Together, the gradual change of the atmospheric conditions, the smell of the first water of the rain (called *xareed*), and the wind characterize saxansaxo. Specialists have tried to explain the saxansaxo phenomenon by conducting experiments on the soil and the plants surrounding the area in question. They found that the smell that characterizes the »saxansaxo moment« originates from the simultaneous combination of the dry land, dry plants, and the contact of the raindrops with the soil and the lightning.[2]

This word is even more important for pastoralists because it is associated with a period of joy and abundance, especially because it means there will be water for livestock for a long period. It creates an awareness of the extent of the territory that the rain would cover in the region, which would be enough to fill all its waterpoints and depressions. Naturally, the precipitation leads to the revival of flora and fauna, with vegetation covering large areas for pasture. The complete transformation of the landscape and habitat gives pastoralists a sense that nature returns to its beauty. This broad-reaching rain would definitely reduce their long journeys to find water and allow grazing for livestock, thereby bringing relief and prosperity.

In fact, for the pastoralist, saxansaxo is more than a pleasant wind that blows and changes the landscape that deeply affects their livelihoods. It is an awakening instant of their minds to forthcoming social and economic development. It reminds them that the time is coming for their awaited social gatherings, like those of the elders for consultations, celebrations, offerings, and marriages. More importantly, it leads to more time for family togetherness, which in the nomadic lifestyle is very rare and precious. Saxansaxo also announces peace with other pastoral communities because saxansaxo comes with a long period of abundance that prevents conflicts with other communities, most of which are caused by watering and grazing their respective livestock. Thus, based on their historic experiences in the past, it paves the path for a period of stability and harmony, and social relief.

The word saxansaxo is also used as a good presage among agro-pastoralists who are the second category of the rural population; farmers. It corresponds to heavy rains coming with the prospect of good seasonal crops with bountiful vegetables and milk production even before the farm harvest. Saxansaxo assures them that at the end of the season, the silos will be filled with cereals and other crops, which certainly increase their purchasing power. It will give them the possibility of getting supplies and agricultural materials, as well as the capacity of expanding their farmlands.

Although the arrival of saxansaxo is less important for the livelihood in the urban center, it nonetheless carries the aforementioned affective dimension. Indeed, saxansaxo appears in a number of poems and songs as a metaphor for an auspicious prediction, but it also refers to people who are awaited, who announce something that one has longed for, like the rain and its relief. Furthermore, many business and media outlets use the word in their brand names to attract clients, and to give a good impression of the qualities of their products and services.

Saxansaxo is useful to this lexicon because it qualifies, with one word, a moment that many language groups try to grasp. The period before the rain evokes different things, such as peace and tranquility like in the expression »the calm before the storm,« referring to a kind of tension or a heavy atmosphere before it rains. In fact, in working on a common vocabulary, is this publication, like saxansaxo, the sign that a longed-for social relief might be in sight?

1 The choice of the Latin alphabet was facilitated by the education system of the colonial period, which was based on either Italian or English.

2 See https://www.bbc.com/somali/war-44992228. (accessed January 29, 2021).

¡Tomá mate!
¡Tomá mate!
¡Tomá mate!
¡Tomá mate!
¡Tomá mate!
¡Tomá mate!
¡Tomá mate!
¡Tomá mate!
¡Tomá mate!
¡Tomá mate!

¡Tomá mate!
Responses to an invitation

Giuliana Kiersz

For me, *mate* means all those obvious and kind of cheesy things like companionship – with myself or others. Nowadays, working from home, something very beautiful happens with my colleagues. Every time we have a meeting, each of us prepares a mate and I have the feeling that we are in the same circle that we used to be part of in the office. For me it's something very intimate; I don't share it. Who doesn't know mate, to any latte prays.[1] For me it's quite a ceremony. It's my favorite time of the day, reading the newspaper. I drink it bitter and when it's lost its flavor. With my mom, with honey. With other people, always bitter. When I'm by myself, bitter; but recently it started to give me heartburn so I've started putting honey in again, and citrus peel. I don't drink it that much because it increases my anxiety. I moved to Uruguay, where I acquired a university culture about what a mate is, how to make a mate, the respect that the yerba deserves. For me mate is everything. I measure the difficulty of my final exams in mate thermoses. For me, drinking mate changed its meaning during my eating disorder. I didn't like it that much until I started using it to make me feel full when I was hungry. Eventually I recovered and now I drink it when I crave the taste, but it still reminds me of those times. The most important things that go through my head come to me in the morning with a mate in my hand. For me, mate is a hug that you don't want to let go of. I'm not much of a mate drinking person, so I don't think my testimony will help you. Mate for me is my uncle before going to sleep at night. It is a way to recognize yourself in others when they drink it. It is asking a stranger for something as intimate as sharing a straw without that being weird. I drink mate by myself, in the early morning, sitting on the couch and looking at the backyard. For me it's very popular because of the fact that it's cheap. My husband and I used to prepare mate for ourselves in the morning and we would start talking, solving our problems while drinking mate. It has an enormous strength to resist over the years. People just want mate, not mate flavored sweets or mate flavored sodas. Drink mate![2] It's a companionship, for sure. Partly a friend. Partly my grandmother. It's been very strange not sharing it this year. And I believe Uruguayans need to stop saying that mate is theirs; they don't produce yerba. You feel an aura, a sense of presence, an aromatic connection that brings you back to earth and to a complicity with yourself and with whom you're sharing it. Is there anything more disgusting than a mate done wrong? A friend said that the first time you put the kettle on to drink mate by yourself, you are an adult. Mate for me is the last thing I still have. Thank you for asking, but it's difficult. Two things come to my mind, on the one hand heartburn and on the other one of the most beautiful encounters that I have with myself. We are talking about drinking mate by oneself, right? Drinking mate with friends is another thing. That's why I'm saying it's quite contradictory but those two things happen to me with mate. Anyway, I hope something from all this works for you.

Para mi el mate significa todas las cosas obvias y medio cursis del orden de la compañia, con uno mismo o con otres. Hoy en día, trabajando desde casa, pasa algo muy hermoso con mis compañeros y compañeras. Cada vez que tenemos una reunión, cada unx se prepara el mate y a mí me da la sensación de que estamos en la misma ronda que compartíamos en la oficina. Para mí es algo íntimo, yo no lo comparto. Quien no conoce el mate a cualquier latte le reza. Para mí es toda una ceremonia. Es mi momento preferido del dia. Leyendo el diario. Lo tomo amargo y lavado. Yo con mi vieja, con miel. Con otras personas siempre amargo. Y cuando estoy sola amargo pero hace poco me empezó a dar mucha acidez entonces le estoy volviendo a poner miel y cascaritas de cítricos. Yo no tomo mucho porque me potencia la ansiedad. Yo me fui a vivir a uruguay y ahí adquirí una cultura universitaria de lo que es un mate, de cómo se prepara un mate, del respeto que se le tiene a la yerba. Para mi el mate es todo. Mido la dificultad de mis finales en termos de mate. Para mí el mate cambió de significado durante mi desorden alimenticio. No me gustaba mucho hasta que lo empecé a usar para llenarme cuando tenía hambre. Eventualmente recuperada, ahora lo tomo cuando se me antoja el gusto, pero sigue recordándome de esas épocas. Las cosas más importan tes que pasan por mi cabeza me pasan a la mañana con un mate en la mano. Para mí el mate es un abrazo que no querés soltar. Yo no soy mucho de tomar mate, no creo que te sirva mi testimonio. El mate para mi es mi tio a la noche antes de irse a dormir. Es reconocerse en otres cuando lo toman. Es pedirle a une extrañe algo tan íntimo como compartir una bombilla sin que sea raro. Tomo mates sola, a la mañana temprano, sentada en el sillon y mirando el patio. Para mi es muy popular por eso, es barato. Con mi marido nos preparábamos un mate a la mañana y ahí nos poníamos a hablar, a resolver los problemas tomando mate. Tiene una fuerza enorme para resistir a traves de los años. La gente solo quiere mate, no golosinas de mate ni gaseosas de mate. ¡Toma mate! Es una compañía sin dudas. Un poco un amigue. Un poco mi abuela también. Este año fue extrañísimo no compartirlo. Y creo que los uruguayos tienen que dejar de decir que el mate es de ellos, ellos no producen yerba. Sentís un aura, un clima de presencia, una aromática conexión, que te vuelve a la tierra y a una complicidad con vos mismx o con quienes lo estés compartiendo. ¿Hay algo más feo que un mate que sale mal? Un amigo decía que la primera vez que ponés la pava para tomar mate solo/a ya sos grande. El mate para mi es lo último que me queda. Gracias por preguntarme, pero es difícil. Se me vienen a la cabeza dos cosas, por un lado acidez y por otro lado uno de los encuentros más lindos que tengo conmigo misma. Estamos hablando de tomarse un mate sola ¿no? Tomar un mate con amigos es otra cosa. Por eso te digo, es bastante contradictoria pero me pasan esas dos cosas con el mate. En fin, espero te sirva de algo todo esto.

1 From the phrase »Who doesn't know God, to any saint prays,« meaning who doesn't know what's good, conforms to anything.

2 From the expression »¡Tomá mate!,« a reply to news that causes surprise.

Wykombinować
Wykombinować
Wykombinować
Wykombinować
Wykombinować
Wykombinować
Wykombinować
Wykombinować

Wykombinować

Wojtek Ziemilski

Wykombinować is one of the key terms of Polish identity. It allows us to go through tough times and still manage life. It means coming up with something (a solution, an idea) in a smart, informal, improvised way, not following the rules. It suggests the situation may have seemed hopeless, but someone persevered and managed to find a solution. You can wykombinować some money, a lunch, something, anything; but you can also wykombinować how to help, or which way to go.

The root verb is *kombinować* – meaning not »to combine,« but rather to contrive, as well as to be up to no good, to cheat, to flout the rules. This can sometimes be pejorative, but is often about bypassing the system to think out of the box. If you succeed – you may wykombinować (come up with) something, outsmarting the encountered reality.

Wykombinować is less about linguistics and more about Polish cultural heritage. It is born out of Polish history and the way we have managed to cope with apparently insurmountable obstacles. It's a survival strategy that became a powerful intellectual and effective weapon we use every day. Take life under the so-called »socialist« regime. How do you find food for your family if the store shelves are literally empty? You have to wykombinować something. Go to another store, wait in a queue with the hope of something popping up, bribe someone. My relatives would sometimes go from Warsaw to the village their family was from to buy an entire pig. All they needed to do, then, was to wykombinować how to transport it back home in their tiny Fiat 126p, packed with family members. This spirit of peculiar entrepreneurship didn't fade after 1989. If anything, it gained new flavors – from illegal businesses to an ever-surprising spirit of independence.

One possible translation to English would be »to figure out.« But for heaven's sake, to figure out has this moving out of a figure, like solving a riddle – from a Polish perspective figuring out sounds somewhat naïve, as if life were a mathematical equation. Like you need to be the good student who finds the correct answer. Wykombinować, on the other hand, doesn't aim for perfection or an objective truth. Rather, it accepts the limited horizon we function within. There may or may not be a final truth. What we need is to come up with strategies of survival and new, creative ways of functioning in this world. Improvise, rethink, persevere, prove them wrong, find a solution, make it work. Somehow.

It does feel like magic. Or alchemy. It's a post-socialist alchemy – you combine things, thoughts, bits and pieces of ideas, you stare into the almost-nothing you have inherited from reality, and somehow you arrive at something which works. It shouldn't have: there was really not enough in the pot, and yet, magically, the solution is here. The strange ingredients you used, the surprising combinations, only make sense once the result appears in hindsight. It was impossible to plan. To be clear – there is nothing esoteric about it. Your knowledge and preparation helped, but you needed to be present here and now, to pierce, to puncture the opaque horizon of possibilities.

One big question is – if someone wykombinowaćs something, »figured something out,« can you emulate it? Possibly. Sometimes wykombinować brings about a recipe. Quite often, however, it is so connected to the perseverance of an individual or group that it remains unique. The pragmatic alchemist's achievement is not easy to repeat. What is clear, however, is that it sets the tone. If someone has done it, it is possible. It's a contagious attitude.

Wykombinować is not some insane sacrifice. It's not connected to a painful effort. You do it because you're up to it. If the problem is serious, you need to focus more and it will take more time. But you don't whine; you don't cry.

Actually – you don't suffer. No more *per aspera ad astra* (Latin for »through the hardships to the stars.«) You replace the cult of suffering with a playful search for solutions. (As a Pole, I can tell you this is a crucial quality for me.)

One last thing: the future.

Wykombinować goes against all the grand narratives. It laughs in the face of governments and corporations. It doesn't mind the stupidity of the future and the seeming lack of perspectives. It looks for solutions, without pathos and great agendas. It may not solve the climate crisis. And a few other issues. But it helps us have hope on a human level. Combining, recombining, outcombining, drilling our way through, every time.

1 The English verb »to combine« had a similar meaning in the eighteenth century. Adam Smith wrote, »But whoever imagines, upon this account, that masters rarely *combine*, is as ignorant of the world as of the subject. Masters are always and everywhere in a sort of tacit, but constant and uniform, *combination*, not to raise the wages of labour above their actual rate.« (italics mine) However, this type of *combining* faded into oblivion, as English lacked the fantastic prefix wy-, which marks a move from a shady activity to a eureka moment. Adam Smith: *An Inquiry Into the Nature and Cause of Wealth of Nations*, Edinburgh 1827, p. 28.

Xapiri
Xapiri
Xapiri
Xapiri
Xapiri
Xapiri
Xapiri
Xapiri
Xapiri
Xapiri

Xapiri

Cássio Diniz Santiago

The ways of organizing this society in which we live – or rather the society called the Western world – need urgent revision and radical change. The predatory culture that permeates the world and aims only at profit logic without considering serious social consequences narrows the possible perspectives that can bring new forms of existence and new possibilities of organization. Adult humans act like children who do not understand what they see, the big picture, and therefore cannot access the *Xapiri* spirits and the sense of responsibility for the current state of affairs. With an arrogance inherited from different moments in Western cultural history, it is impossible to understand the problems and difficulties that world citizens have to face. It seems foolish to try to preserve our own lives by destroying life itself. Considering that at the moment children are taking the leading places of responsibility, it seems that adults lost access to the world of the Xapiri spirits a long time ago.

Xapiri spirits are what is called knowledge, but they are also living knowledge and living entities, even if they are understood as images. So you could call them living images. Xapiri spirits neither separate knowledge from affection, nor technology from existence. Everything that has been separated in Western culture is connected in the Xapiri spirits. It is therefore a knowledge that does not even need the word transdisciplinary, because it is inherently so from the beginning.

How is possible that a culture like the Yanomami, which for thousands of years has preserved its environment on the Amazon without leaving a trace, and most of all possesses deep knowledge on how to live better, be neglected as primitive? How can the phantom words of our books and our lost memory take the place of life itself and distort perception so that inanimate, industrial, and conceptual objects take the place of living beings themselves?

We are ruled by cans of beer or cars; no longer by gods or Xapiri spirits. The symbolic universe was transferred to objects that are the result of the destruction of life. They are objects of destruction because it is not possible to be governed by objects that need our own blood to exist, because it is our blood that feeds the machines, which in turn depend on the extraction of minerals among other forms of devastation.

The loss of contact with the Xapiri spirits and with the universe that Western culture calls symbolic, has created the rigidity of these objects produced to replace life's impermanence and fragility. Yes, through technology there is an immense capacity for communication, but current Western communication seems to be a Tower of Babel. In this Tower, the problem may not be the different languages, but the fact that nobody listens to each other.

For that, Xapiri spirits are the image-beings that accompany every moment, every gesture, every passage, and

Cássio Diniz Santiago, *Sudden dream of the reason*, pencil on paper, 2021
Courtesy of the artist

that have their own wisdom in protecting us, in being angry with us, in accompanying every small gesture of nature. It is the spirits that accompany the reading of this text. Xapiri spirits cannot be translated, but conditions can be created for them to visit us and thus even without a possible translation, we can understand them. And, perhaps in this way the Xapiri can find their way back, to dance for us within our dreams, offering their protection and wisdom.

As Davi Kopenawa says, »Your children need to learn to dream. Dream on this path to walk, fight, and speak together against destructive men. Because destructive men are many. They are powerful *marea sikï*. *Marea sikï* means money. We Indigenous people, we live without money. To this day we live without money. Our money is food. Food for the people who use the wealth of *Maxita-Uhiri*. Take care, not to let it be destroyed, not to let our forest be deforested. Do not let the destruction of our rivers, our streams, our health, our beauty of the great soul of *Maxita-Uhiri* happen.«

The work of Davi Kopenawa and Bruce Albert in the book *The Falling Sky: Words of a Yanomami Shaman* is an example of listening. The book offers an opportunity to listen to Yanomami culture, which has been preserved aurally and where words are not detached from context, as they are in Western culture.

Evidently, in some way, each word transported from one context to another through writing is untranslatable.

The experiences of life are untranslatable through written words. It is necessary to live an experience, and not only to read about it. It is known that only those who have been through this or that can understand this or that. This is a common expression in this world that we call the world, but there are many different worlds, and right now, many of them are disappearing while others are being created.

The dance of creation and destruction seems far from our influence, but it is performed by each one of us at every moment. Questioning assumptions that are considered fundamental, asking not only what the concept is, but what the concept of the concept is, crossing the veil of illusion built by reason over time, is perhaps a way of authorizing different ways of life to be alive.

XIN

XIN

XIN

NIX

NIX

NIX

NIX

XIN

XIN

XIN
信
Dong Li

The nineteenth-century scholar YAN Fu (严复) admirably laid out the most influential Chinese translation theories, and the first principle is *XIN* (信). XIN means »trustworthy of what the text says.« Obviously, this principle demands that the translation be faithful to the original. However, this is often problematic when it comes to idioms and poetic images. Inspired by the French philosopher Paul Ricoeur's idea of untranslatability and approximation, I would, by way of anecdotes, propose a new interpretation of XIN as »authenticity.«

In his book *On Translation*,[1] Ricoeur introduces notions of translation as »work of mourning« and »work of remembering.« For Ricoeur, languages are *a priori* untranslatable into each other. However, this is not a point of despair, but rather one of acceptance and possibility. As the translator »mourns« the inevitable loss of the original text, s/he also »remembers« the vision of the text and imparts, or more technically, »approximates« it into another language. Herein lies a kind of »linguistic hospitability« – welcoming the foreign text into the home of another language.

Ricoeur highlights some of the fundamental questions in translation that resonate with me as a literary translator. Should I translate an idiom literally into a hodgepodge of words that might not make much sense in the receiving culture, so that the foreignness could be preserved? What about an image in a poem that sets off a constellation of associations in the original text, but becomes bland in the target language, if rendered word for word? How do we, in our everyday practice, »mourn« a text and its departing culture, and let a translated text »remember« in the receiving culture? The more I contemplate this, the more inadequate I find the interpretation of XIN as faithfulness and trustworthiness.

From my experience, rather than faithfully translating an idiom into a literal word-hoard, a transformation of the idiom to a comparable one that evokes similar meaning or emotion might be a solution. Similarly, an image should ignite close feelings or intensity for the reader in both cultures. In this way, the translated text could stay approximately true, or in other words, authentic.

Take this line from the Chinese poet Zhu Zhu, which I have translated into English.

我	看见	过	生活	的	全部	色彩。
I	see	past indicator	life	's	all	colors

My translation: I saw all the brilliance of this life.

The context of this line is wind blowing every curtain on the street, and the poet reflects and has a revelation. »Colors« sounds either bland, or a bit unclear, as to whether it denotatively refers to »true meaning« or »intentions.« What Zhu Zhu meant here is in fact straightforward, »colors« in the sense of wonderful things in life. Instead of »colors,« »brilliance« might be a quick fix to the problem. »Brilliance« is not a literal translation of the original, but stands closer to the original in its emotional impact. Here's another line from Zhu Zhu:

> ... 从 任何 / 博物馆 的 窗口 向
> ... from any / museum 's window toward
>
> 外 看, 总是 美丽的。
> outside see always beautiful
>
> My translation: peering / from every
> museum window, it is beautiful out and out.

The challenge here is not about choosing the most appropriate word, rather, how to make this typical line from Zhu Zhu understatedly poetic. A literal translation in English seems lackluster. In this poem, Zhu Zhu is making a statement that Chinese poets should not be expected to just write political poetry, and there is so much openness that one does not see in contemporary Chinese poetry. I added »and out« after the first »out« to emphasize this yearning for this openness, but also to give the line a kind of strangeness that draws attention. This add-on literally adds an effect that might not be obvious in the original, but this emotive force of the poem demands a special treatment.

The last example is from an innovative use of an idiom from another contemporary Chinese poet Zang Di, which I, with the poet Lea Schneider, have translated into German. The idiom

狗 血 喷 头
dog blood gush head

normally means to overwhelm somebody with reproaches. With humor, Zang Di breaks this idiom and adds a turkey to the party:

狗 的 舌头 上 / 火鸡 也 会 喷 血？
dog 's tongue on turkey also can gush blood

With no one-to-one counterpart in German, the closest we could find is another idiom *jemandem etwas um die Ohren hauen*, literally in English, »to knock something around somebody's ears.« To add a bit of humor to this, Lea put »a bag of rice« in German, *einen Sack Reis* in the mix for emphasis, thus we have *einen Sack Reis schnell um die Ohren gehauen kriegt*; literally in English, »to quickly have a bag of rice knocked around the ears.«

The playful »turkey on a dog's tongue« turns into »a bag of rice« with both meaning and humor preserved. Languages sometimes work out their own magic. If translated literally, it would not make sense, and worse still, the reader might be totally lost.

As a translator, if I conform entirely to the original text and to the interpretation of YAN Fu's first principle, XIN, as faithfulness, translation would be not only impossible but also a constant source of total despair. Ricoeur's meditation on translation as a kind of »linguistic hospitality« presumes the impossibility of the literal rendition between languages, and by accepting it as the basic condition of translation, opens up new room for translators to engage and even play with the text to the extent that meanings and feelings are imparted and thus become possible. It is time to read XIN not as trustworthy of what the text says, but rather, as authentic to what the original text truly conveys. In other words, it is time to shift the reading of XIN from faithfulness to authenticity.

1 Paul Ricoeur: *Sur la traduction*, Paris 2004.

yaʿṭīkī-l-ʿāfī
yaʿṭīke-l-ʿāfī
yaʿṭīkī-l-ʿāfī
yaʿṭīke-l-ʿāfī
yaʿṭīkī-l-ʿāfī
yaʿṭīke-l-ʿāfī
yaʿṭīkī-l-ʿāfī
yaʿṭīke-l-ʿāfī
yaʿṭīkī-l-ʿāfī

ya'ṭīkī-l-'āfī feminine

يعطيكي العافية

ya'ṭīke-l-'āfī masculine

يعطيك العافية

Haneen Naamneh

When I walk past construction workers near my street, or buy my loaf from the neighborhood bakery, or watch teachers lead children into their schools in the mornings, or knock on the doors of administration employees, I find myself, now living in Europe, digging deep into English idioms searching for words of apperception. Words that would be comparable to the meaning of the Arabic term *yaʿṭīkī-l-ʿafī* to express my gratitude, appreciation, and respect to those who work tirelessly every day.

Instead, I only say thanks with a big smile. But thanks is not even close to the meaning of yăʿṭīkī-l-ʿăfī! The closest translation would be »May God give you health and wellness.« Yet the word connotes much more than mere health. Rather, it is a wish for prolonging perseverance and the physical ability to work and produce. It stems from the strength and determination of the body and soul to give and work. (Arabic has its own terms for wishing health to someone ill, but there's no room for that here.)

While it is a wish addressing God, yăʿṭīkī-l-ʿăfī is a social idiom that everyone uses, regardless of religion, age, or gender. Whether it is yăʿṭīkī-l-ʿăfī (feminine) or yăʿṭīke-l-ʿăfī (masculine), all work, domestic or otherwise, deserves to be regarded. The phrase also abolishes classes and makes the concept of work and production of various kinds a collective social activity, in which everyone's efforts and work are equally appreciated.

In fact, the beauty of yăʿṭīkī-l-ʿăfī lies in its intimacy, which immediately dissipates the alienation that exists between strangers. Saying it means appreciating the efforts of someone who helps, builds, creates, and produces the conditions that allow us to be, together, in this public space. It also extends to the private space, as saying it draws us closer to those with whom we share our domesticity – partners or parents; siblings or roommates. We would also say yăʿṭīkī-l-ʿăfī to those with whom we collegially and reciprocally work.

Yăʿṭīkī-l-ʿăfī is also used as a salute to greet someone when entering a shop or approaching someone during her work. It replaces hello, hi, and other greetings; it becomes both a greeting and an appreciation. Ironically, that appreciation may be turned upside-down if yăʿṭīkī-l-ʿăfī is said in anger or sarcasm. It then becomes a phrase to reprimand someone for a mistake or a bad product, for example cutting a piece of wood to the wrong measurements or adding sugar instead of salt to a soup.

In all its conditions, yăʿṭīkī-l-ʿăfī keeps reminding me of the meaning of home, bestowal, and hard work, when other languages fail to do so. This meaning travels beyond the geographies and imageries of the Arabic language, rendering yăʿṭīkī-l-ʿăfī universal as much as communal.

Photo: Mohamed Badarne
Courtesy of the photographer

Appendix

Introduction, p. 6

Elke aus dem Moore
has been the director of Akademie Schloss Solitude since 2018. Previously, she headed the art department of the ifa (Institut für Auslandsbeziehungen) and was responsible for the international exhibition program as director of the Künstlerhaus Stuttgart from 2003 to 2006. From 1999 to 2002 she was curator for contemporary art at the Shedhalle Zurich. She studied literature and art in Osnabrück, Zurich, and Bochum.

Introduction, p. 6

Denise Helene Sumi
is a curator and editor based in Vienna and Stuttgart. As part of Akademie Schloss Solitude's Digital Solitude team she is responsible for editing the Solitude Journal and the Solitude Blog as well as partly for the Web Residency program. She is a founding member and codirector of the exhibition space Kevin Space in Vienna.

Introduction, p. 6

Lara Treffeisen
graduated in literature, arts, and media studies from University of Konstanz and Boğaziçi Üniversitesi, Istanbul. After that, she worked at Staatsgalerie Stuttgart and ifa (Institut für Auslandsbeziehungen). Since completing her master's degree in cultural studies and cultural management, she works as a trainee at Akademie Schloss Solitude.

Foreword, p. 16

Kübra Gümüşay
is the author of the bestselling non-fiction book *Sprache und Sein (Language und Being)*, published by Hanser Berlin in spring 2020. She is cofounder of eeden, a feminist co-creation space in Hamburg, as well as numerous campaigns and associations – including the anti-racism campaign #SchauHin; the feminist alliance #ausnahmslos, which was awarded the Clara Zetkin Women's Award in 2016; and the campaign »Organisierte Liebe« (Organized Love). She is a fellow of the Progressive Center and Associate Expert at the Center for Intersectional Justice. Her blog, »ein-fremdwoerterbuch.com« was nominated for the Grimme Online Award in 2011. In 2018, *Forbes* magazine ranked her among the top 30 under 30 in Europe in media and marketing.

A

Anta(h)shira, p. 26
অন্তঃশীরা

Raqs Media Collective
was formed in 1992 by Jeebesh Bagchi, Monica Narula, and Shuddhabrata Sengupta. The word »raqs« in several languages denotes an intensification of awareness and presence attained by whirling, turning, being in a state of revolution. Raqs Media Collective takes this sense to mean »kinetic contemplation« and a restless and energetic entanglement with the world, and with time. Raqs practices across several media; making installation, sculpture, video, performance, text, lexica, and curation. Their work finds them at the intersection of contemporary art, philosophical speculation, and historical inquiry. They were the artistic directors of *Afterglow*, the recently concluded Yokohama Triennale 2020.

Avos', p. 32

Viktoria Morasch
is a journalist and writer based in Berlin. She was born in the Soviet Union and moved to Germany when she was two years old. Russian was her first language, but once she grew older, she realized that her Russian skills remained at an elementary level. Chaning this fact is one of her life goals.

Axé, p. 38

Vinicius Jatobá
is a Latin-American writer born in Brazil. A curator, theater director, and producer, he writes fiction and nonfiction, and for the stage. After completing residencies at Cité des Arts (Paris) and Akademie Schloss Solitude (Stuttgart), he is currently an artist-in-residence at Theatre Freiburg.

B

Bayanihan, p. 46

Mica Cabildo
is an artist and designer based in Metro Manila, Philippines. She studied advertising, worked in visual communications, and trained in printmaking. She was a Solitude

fellow for design in 2014–15 and has since undertaken residencies at Sapporo Tenjinyama Art Studio (Sapporo/JP), Schleswig-Holsteinisches Künstlerhaus (Eckernförde/DE), Akiyoshidai International Art Village (Yamaguchi/JP), and Gasworks (London/UK). Mica makes prints, installations, and community art activities about climate, landscape, and ecology.

Bezmetic, p. 54
Edith Lázár
is an art writer and (unprofessional) fashion theorist based in Cluj-Napoca, Romania. She has a background in art history and is a dropout academic in the field of philosophy. Her research and wanderings focus on fictions, aesthetic politics, speculative design, and the sociopolitical threads of fashion. She is the cofounder and part of the curatorial collective Aici Acolo and she was a design/fashion theory fellow at Akademie Schloss Solitude in 2019. Her soft spots are science fiction, eerie words, secondhand clothes, and mangoes.

C

Cocok, p. 62
Laura Romano
is a teacher in the fields of languages, yoga, and meditation. She also has experience in commerce, fashion, and interior design, as well as in garden landscaping. Romano was born and raised in Italy and has a master's degree in philosophy. Since 1979 she has been living in Solo, Central Java, Indonesia. There she got in touch with the Sumarah meditation tradition and many of its teachers. Since 1995, Romano has been teaching Sumarah meditations outside Indonesia, mainly in Europe. She published a book on the subject, *Sumarah – Spiritual Wisdom from Java*, which is available in English, Italian, and German.

F

Filotimo, p. 68
Philotimo
Φιλότιμο
Alkistis Thomidou
born in 1984 in Thessaloniki, is a Berlin-based architect. She holds a diploma in architecture and a master's degree in urban design from the ETH Zurich. In her work, she investigates the built environment across multiple scales in its social, economical, and structural components through design and interdisciplinary research. She is interested in collecting alternative city-making narratives and protocols and collective approaches, while developing open spatial frameworks inspired by the inventiveness of everyday life. She is cofounder of forty-five degrees, an architecture and urban design practice currently in search of emerging »rituals« and their potential to shape radical practices of commoning along the 45-degree North parallel.

G

Gostopriemstvo, p. 76
Остоприемство
Alexander Manuiloff
is a prizewinning writer, playwright, and screenwriter of Bulgarian origin whose theatrical works have been invited to important theater festivals and venues on four continents. Manuiloff's dramaturgy has so far been translated into thirteen languages and is already studied in some university programs, (e.g. Georgetown University in the United States). After Manuiloff's 2017 tour to Washington at ForumTheatre/Woolly Mammoth, the *DC Theatre Scene* called him »a rare creator«, the *Washington Post* found his piece »exceptionally thoughtful«, while the *Broadway World* defined Manuiloff's writing as being »akin to magical realism.«

Gurukulam, p. 84
Prasanna Oommen
has been working for 20 years as a public relations officer, moderator (German/English), and author in the fields of culture, education, digitization, urban development, development and cooperation, migration, diversity, and media. She was a press spokesperson for various institutions in North-Rhine Westphalia and Hessen, and is a former board member and active member for Neue Deutsche Medienmacher e.V., a media nonprofit. Furthermore, she is a trained classical dancer (Cologne, Bangalore) and has worked for many years in arts education for children and adults. In 2020 she was the juror and mentor for

the Digital Cultural Journalism and New Media fellowship program at the Akademie Schloss Solitude in Stuttgart.

I

Innigkeit, p. 94

Regina Dürig

born 1982 in Mannheim, Germany, is a Switzerland-based writer, performer, lecturer, and researcher. She has published miniatures, short stories, audio dramas, children's books, and young adult novels. She closely collaborates with the musician Christian Müller in the experimental story and sound duo Butterland, and with artists in other disciplines, notably Patrizia Bach. Dürig's writings have won several awards, including the IBBY Honour List, the Wartholz Literature Prize, the Peter-Haertling-Preis, and the Literature Prize of the Canton of Berne. She was a fellow at Akademie Schloss Solitude in 2018.

Innigkeit, p. 94

Patrizia Bach

is a visual artist living and working in Berlin. Her main artistic medium is drawing, and her work focuses on topics such as archiving, collecting, and re-arranging; as well as approaching the city as a site of memory, history, and storage. For the past decade, she has been focusing on long-term projects that include in-depth research processes, which result in expansive drawing installations that take over architecture. She works in several interdisciplinary collaborations, notably with Regina Dürig. Bach has received numerous scholarships and was a fellow at Akademie Schloss Solitude in 2018.

J

Juogi, p. 110

Enos Nyamor

is an art writer, cultural journalist, and cultural critic. Born and raised in Nairobi and a former Akademie Schloss Solitude fellow, Enos is currently an MFA Art Writing candidate at New York City's School of Visual Arts. Some of his past writings and projects focused on the intersection between physical movement and digital migration, as well as site-specific elements in live art. He is presently working on a collection of essays on intersubjectivity in computer-generated images and dimensions of new media experiences.

L

Langar, p. 118

Simar Preet Kaur

is a writer based in the Indian Himalayas. Her features and narrative essays have appeared in a range of publications including *Commonwealth Writers*, *National Geographic Traveler*, *Stand Magazine*, and *Papercuts*. Simar received a Sangam House Fellowship in 2015 and the Charles Wallace Fellowship in Creative Writing at University of Stirling, Scotland, in 2016. She spent 2018 at Akademie Schloss Solitude on a year-long literature fellowship, working on her first book set on a high mountain road.

M

Mapalus, p. 126

Natasha Tontey

is an artist and graphic designer based in Yogyakarta. She is interested in exploring the concept of fiction as a method of speculative thinking. Her works have been shown at transmediale for refusal (2021), Asian Film Archive (2021), Kyoto Experiment (2021), Other Futures: Multispecies Experiment (2019), Polyphonic Social by Liquid Architecture (2019), and The Wrong Biennale (2019), among others. Tontey received the HASH Award 2020 for Net-Based Projects in the Fields of Art, Technology, and Design by ZKM | Karlsruhe and Akademie Schloss Solitude.

Micchāmi Dukkaḍaṃ, p. 132

Nishant Shah

is a feminist, humanist, and technologist. He is Director of Research & Outreach and Professor of Aesthetics and Cultures of Technology at ArtEZ University of the Arts, the Netherlands. He was the cofounder of the Centre for Internet & Society, India, and is a 2020–21 Faculty Associate at the Berkman Klein Center for Internet & Society at Harvard University. He serves as a knowledge partner with the Dutch social justice organization HIVOS on their art-technology program *Digital Earth* and with the Feminist

Internet Research Network. Shah's current work addresses questions of misinformation, fakeness, and humane futures of our digital conditions.

O

Oisiveté, p. 140

Jérôme Toussaint
graduated from Université libre de Bruxelles, Belgium, with degrees in law (2007) and performance studies (2012). He works as a lawyer and legal researcher in German and Belgian law, and is also a certified translator. Toussaint was a fellow at the Akademie in the discipline of Jurisprudence/Law.

S

Sahaja, p. 146

Vipul Rikhi
is a writer, singer, poet, storyteller, and translator, immersed in the oral traditions of Kabir and other Bhakti and Sufi poets for more than a decade. He is the author of several books of poetry, fiction, and translation. His most recent book is *One Palace, A Thousand Doorways*, a book of translations of mystic poetry. His work with the Kabir Project has involved writing, translations, research, curations, and the creation of a vast digital archive called Ajab Shahar. He sings mystic poetry in the folk music traditions and performs internationally. He was a fellow for literature at the Akademie Schloss Solitude.

Saxansaxo, p. 154

Abukar Mursal and Faduma Abukar
are based respectively in Neuchâtel, Switzerland and Berlin, Germany. They are a father-daughter duo who share a passion for languages and their translations. Both speak many languages including English, French, and Somali, and they share a passion for words – both their etymologies and social contexts, as well as word plays.

T

¡Tomá mate!, p. 162

Giuliana Kiersz
born 1991 in Buenos Aires, is a writer, playwright, and artist. Her work explores our relationship with language, analyzing what language itself collects and how we can collectively express our emotions and experiences to reflect on difference through the lens of sameness. As part of her investigations, she has organized writing gatherings in different contexts around the world. These are sensitive and political spaces in which to reflect on the territories we collectively inhabit. Her texts have been translated into English, French, and Portuguese and are published by Rara Avis Editorial, Libros del Rojas, Fondo Editorial ENSAD, Editorial INTeatro, Espejo Somos, and Libros Drama.

W

Wykombinować, p. 170

Wojtek Ziemilski
is a theater director and visual artist. His performances have been shown in more than twenty countries at events such as the Ruhrtriennale or the Prague Quadriennial, and have won awards including the main prizes of both the Zürcher Theater Spektakel and the Fast Forward Festival in Dresden. Ziemilski expands and extends the idea of documentary performance, often inquiring into spectatorship and the possibility of action. He teaches contemporary approaches to performance with a particular focus on devising techniques, connections between contemporary dance and theater, and the use of media in performance. He is a lecturer at the National Academy of Dramatic Art in Warsaw and at Warsaw University, and has given lectures and workshops across the world.

X

Xapiri, p. 176

Cássio Diniz Santiago
born 1973 in São Paulo, Brazil, is a performance artist, theater and dance director, dramaturg, and researcher. He earned his bachelor's degree in performing arts at the State University of Campinas, Brazil and from 2017 to 2019, studied choreography and performance at Giessen University in Germany. His performance, theater, dance, and multidisciplinary art projects have been presented at the São Paulo Biennial, Modern Art Museum of São Paulo, Baltic Circle International Theatre Festival, Akademie der Künste, Kunstlerhaus Mousonturm, SESC SP, and other venues. In 2015, he

was an *Art, Science, and Business* fellow at Akademie Schloss Solitude. He also works as an educator and curator. He has lived and worked in Germany since 2017.

XIN, p. 184
信
Dong Li
was born and raised in the People's Republic of China. He was educated at Deep Springs College and Brown University. He is a poet of the lost world. For his poems and literary projects, he has received fellowships from Akademie Schloss Solitude, Alexander von Humboldt Foundation, Camargo Foundation, Yaddo, and others. A recipient of the PEN/Heim Translation Grant, Dong Li also translates from the Chinese, English, and German. His translated or co-translated collections have been published or are forthcoming with Deep Vellum/Phoneme Media, Giramondo Publishing, Carl Hanser Verlag, East China Normal University Press, and Shanghai Translation Publishing House.

Y

ya'ṭīkī-l-'āfī (f.), p. 192
ya'ṭīkḗ-l-'āfī (m.)
Haneen Naamneh
is a researcher, writer, and translator. She studied law and sociology in London. She is primarily interested in archives, social history, and food. In 2020, she was a fellow with the Akademie Schloss Solitude and a researcher with the project *Archival City – Bridging Urban Past and Future*. In the past, she worked as a lawyer as well as a researcher at the London School of Economics and Political Science.

Imprint

Untranslatable Terms of Cultural Practices
A Shared Vocabulary

Editor: Elke aus dem Moore

Contributors: Faduma Abukar, Patrizia Bach, Regina Dürig, Mica Cabildo, Vinicius Jatobá, Simar Preet Kaur, Giuliana Kiersz, Dong Li, Edith Lázár, Alexander Manuiloff, Viktoria Morasch, Abukar Mursal, Haneen Naamneh, Enos Nyamor, Prasanna Oommen, Raqs Media Collective, Vipul Rikhi, Laura Romano, Cássio Diniz Santiago, Nishant Shah, Alkistis Thomidou, Natasha Tontey, Jérôme Toussaint, Wojtek Ziemilski

Introduction: Kübra Gümüşay

Editors-in-chief: Denise Helene Sumi and Lara Treffeisen
Associate Editor: Sebastian Schneider
Copy Editing: Kimberly Bradley
Proofreading: Chloe Stead
Translation: Harriet Rössger
Graphic Design: beton.studio, Vienna
Printing and Binding: DZA Druckerei zu Altenburg GmbH

Published by Edition Solitude and Archive Books

Akademie Schloss Solitude
Solitude 3
70197 Stuttgart
Germany
mail@akademie-solitude.de
www.akademie-solitude.de

Archive Books
Reinickendorfer Straße 17
13347 Berlin
Germany
mail@archivebooks.org
www.archivebooks.org

First edition printed in Germany
Edition of 1000 copies

ISBN 978-3-948212-55-1

Untranslatable Terms of Cultural Practices is published in the course of the 30th anniversary of Akademie Schloss Solitude. The anniversary activities of Akademie Schloss Solitude are supported by Wüstenrot Stiftung.

AKADEMIE SCHLOSS SOLITUDE | Archive Books | WÜSTENROT STIFTUNG